ON HISTORICAL AND POLITICAL KNOWING

On
HISTORICAL
and
POLITICAL
KNOWING

*An Inquiry into Some Problems
of Universal Law
&
Human Freedom*

Morton A. Kaplan

The University of Chicago Press
Chicago & London

International Standard Book Number: 0-226-42420-0
Library of Congress Catalog Card Number: 79-131879
The University of Chicago Press, Chicago 60637
The University of Chicago Press, Ltd., London

Contents

Preface

This book is neither a technical treatise nor a systematic work in the philosophy of history. Its origin lies in my interests in scientific method and systems theory as applied to the social sciences, in the roles of theory, universal laws, and accounts of particular events, as well as in more general problems of human freedom. I shall return more specifically to these interests later in the preface and, of course, in the book.

The more I thought about these problems, the more it appeared that many current misconceptions concerning them lie, at least in part, in the realm of philosophy. Many of these misconceptions have a common core that I believe can be clarified by philosophical analysis. Because this is my purpose, I do not care to dilute the insights I hope this book provides, or to lose the readers to whom it is primarily addressed, by a concern with the detailed implications of my positions or with their detailed interrelationships, as important as these tasks undoubtedly would be in a different work. Admittedly, this runs the risk that some topics are covered "once over lightly," but this is the risk that I prefer to take in the effort to help redirect modern social science from some important theoretical mistakes and to save much effort that I believe is wasted. In the process, I hope that some of the insights in this book will be of value even to some whose interests are even more general than mine. The problems I attempt to illuminate include some of the most important and fundamental in the realm of knowing.

Most of our knowledge rests on common sense. In each culture, a common framework of commonsense assumptions permits intersubjective communication among people. This common framework of understanding contains some genuine wisdom (although it is not self-conscious with respect to the parameters that limit its application), some truisms that are applicable and some that are misleading, some tautologies that are not understood as such, and some elements of understanding that are scientific or approach the scientific. Attempts at self-consciousness concerning the limits of the various processes by which knowledge is obtained bring us into the realm of the philosophy of history, of social science, and of science.

The seventeenth-century view of the world was a view of an ordered and deterministic universe that could be completely known by the human mind. A "copy" theory of knowledge was inherent in this world view. The difficulties of that position produced serious philosophic debate; some of the more important figures in this debate were Hume, Kant, Hegel, and Marx. Yet the problems with which they dealt had not been previously unknown in the history of philosophy. The debate between realism and nominalism, for instance, in part turned on this problem.

The "copy" theory of knowledge ignores the contextual and also the self-referring aspects of knowing. The former involve the elliptical character of empirical statements and the fact that such statements are dependent on the instrument of perception as well as upon that which is perceived. Nonetheless, publicly communicable objective knowledge is possible with respect to social and historical knowledge as well as to physical objects. One theme this book deals with this problem and places the sociology of knowledge within a broader philosophical context. The latter problem of the self-referring aspects of knowing involves a number of well-known paradoxes as well as other philosophical difficulties. The core of this latter problem is that the framework within which knowledge occurs can never be included in knowledge itself. Thus, for instance, scientific proof according to the methods of science can never be used to establish the methods of science themselves. The directive rules that govern procedures can never be established by the application of the procedures. Although this self-referring relationship manifests itself differently and with different consequences in the different realms of knowing, the common core of the difficulty eventually obtrudes itself at the limits of knowledge. The difficulty is inherent and cannot be overcome, for even a framework of knowing that comprehended all others and eliminated their difficulties would eventually obtrude its own limitations on knowledge. This is the misleading core of truth in the Platonic assumption that knowledge can only be remembered but not discovered. This Platonic assumption does not deal adequately with the knowledge that stems from negative feedback processes; but it is true that knowledge would be impossible if the process of knowing started with John Locke's *tabula rasa*. Either knowledge inheres in existential being or there can be no knowledge. We can transcend particular limits on knowledge; but we can never know anything "perfectly," for that would involve our transcending the framework within which knowledge is acquired. Indeed, to speak of "limits" on knowledge implies—incorrectly so— that knowing replicates reality rather than reveals it contextually.

Limitations on knowledge occur in a diverse number of realms of inquiry. In the realm of logic and mathematics, Gödel has shown that any mathematical system that can be shown to be consistent is necessarily incomplete in the sense that it cannot be used in principle to prove all true statements involving the symbols in the axioms. The logical paradoxes explored by Bertrand Russell are inherently unsolvable, although they can be avoided by a decision rule such as the theory of types that directs the user not to regard particular kinds of statements as self-referring. Thus, the question whether the class of all classes that include themselves is a member of itself is not a question to be asked according to the theory of types. There is a common core between Gödel's demonstration and Russell's rule: both revolve around a situation in which the framework of knowledge is self-referring. The epistemological problem also involves a problem of self-reference: the fact that the act or state of knowing cannot include itself.

When we enter the realm of empirical science, we eventually meet other limitations. Heisenberg has shown that at the level of subatomic particles position and velocity cannot be known at the same time; they are not simultaneously meaningful. Einstein has shown in the realm of macrophysics that the relationship of independent systems—one the system of the observor and the other the system of the observed—is such that the assertion of simultaneity of time depends upon the adoption of an arbitrary system of reference. It is well known that the use of measuring instruments always involves a range of error; Born has argued that this will produce in some finite sequence a situation in which even a probabilistic prediction is no longer possible. The problems raised in Marxian sociology and in historicism also involve the relationship of the observer to the observed and place certain limits on what can be said.

The principles of limitation of which we are speaking are inherent, although quite often improvements can be made in any existing mode of knowing. Often the limitations are unimportant. For instance, astrophysicists can project the positions of the stars for tens of thousands of years without worrying about measurement errors and their effects upon prediction; for practical purposes their models are fully determined models. In other realms, for instance that of subatomic physics, where the simultaneous determination of position and of velocity is meaningless, the predictive model is considered by some to be lawful in terms of Schrödinger's equations.

As we consider these limits on knowledge, philosophical problems arise. What do we mean by truth, by meaning, by freedom, whether of a particle, of a man, or of an organization? What do we mean by prudence of action in an uncertain world? The chapters that follow attempt to explore these questions with respect to different aspects of the philosohy of history and of social science.

The problems occurring within each framework of discussion are in reality recurring problems that stem from the common core of the limitations upon knowing. They manifest themselves in somewhat different ways in each case, however. The framework of our exploration is given by the philosophy of systemic pragmaticism.[1] The common theme of our answers to the questions raised is that objective knowledge is possible and meaningful, that it involves statements that can be expressed universalistically in the language of science, that nonetheless science is unable to exhaust the infinity of meanings that can be given to the existential world. The historicists and the students of the sociology of knowledge have in my opinion incorrectly transformed this limitation upon knowledge into the fundamental ground for knowledge. Other writers in the philosophy of history have made pertinent challenges to the capacity of science to exhaust the world or to express it adequately but have again overstated the case and transformed a limitation upon knowledge into a much broader and unacceptable principle. Much of the discussion of the problem of the relationship of freedom and determinacy suffers from a similar failure properly to assess the polarities in which thought is trapped by limitations on knowledge. I am under no illusion that I have "solved" this problem, but I hope that I have aided in its clarification.

We will not here pursue—except tangentially and in passing—the claim made in *Macropolitics* that only

1. See the introductory essay in Morton A. Kaplan, *Macropolitics: Essays on the Philosophy and Science of Politics* (Chicago: Aldine Publishing Co., 1969).

the methods of empirical science provide a self-correcting set of publicly communicable rules for arriving at empirical conclusions that are not dependent on any human purpose except that of discovering the truth, that is, of explaining or of finding the meaning of something. Charles Peirce and Morris Cohen developed this argument, and John Dewey wrote at length on it. I do not consider the position refutable that only a scientific philosophy permits publicly communicable knowledge. Although its methods cannot be used to validate themselves, only their acceptance eliminates the need to resort to an increasing series of subsidiary intuitions that cannot be publicly validated.

This inquiry, however, has more specific objectives as well as the general ones noted earlier. In my opinion, historians and political scientists, particularly in the field of international relations, have misperceived each other's objectives. In the essays in *Macropolitics,* I touched on some of the differences between macropolitical and micropolitical analyses and on the fact that even macropolitical analyses are often conducted from different, but equally legitimate, perspectives. For instance, a theory of international politics and a theory of foreign policy select different variables as the focus of analysis.

Some of these issues are treated in this book from a perspective different from that of *Macropolitics—*

from the framework of explanation in history. I agree with Morris Cohen, Carl Hempel, and Karl Popper that explanation in history depends upon laws, either strictly or loosely. In addition, there are important differences in practice, although not in principle, between the problems of macroanalysis and those of microanalysis. In this essay, I touch on some of these issues and attempt to relate them to problems of decision-making and of human freedom.

My view of freedom—nowhere yet achieved on earth—involves a view of the kinds of societies that permit freedom to develop and prosper and of a world in which such societies can prosper. In the present circumstances, many tragic choices are required, but this is a subject about which I appropriately write elsewhere.[2]

The philosophy of systemic pragmaticism, which was developed in *Macropolitics,* permits pragmaticist tests (becoming) to be linked to being in a more satisfactory—and more scientific—manner than is achieved by either existentialism or phenomenalism. This position was further developed in *Dissent and the State* and is carried still further in this book, particularly in chapter 3.

2. See Morton A. Kaplan, *Dissent in the State in Peace and War: An Essay on the Grounds of Public Morality* (New York: Dunellen Co., 1970).

Acknowledgments

I wish to thank Karl Weintraub and Nathan Leites for their careful and helpful reading of the manuscript. Carl G. Hempel was of particular assistance in criticizing those portions of the manuscript dealing with the concept of scientific law. Sidney Hook and Estel Wood Kelly provided detailed and extremely helpful criticisms of the entire manuscript.

ON HISTORICAL AND
POLITICAL KNOWING

1
Knowing and Explaining

Ordinary discourse usually assumes a seventeenth-century Lockean view of the process by means of which knowledge is acquired. There is an external reality and our senses present it to us. Explanation is a process of naive discovery. In contrast with this view, followers of Marx or of Karl Mannheim accept the view that the social or historical understanding of the world is a matter of class or of social position. In its extreme existentialist form, the position is taken that form is imposed by the human mind on external reality, that we play self-imposed roles in the world, and that reality is what we make it, if not an outright fiction.

Both Marx and Mannheim have a contextual theory of social knowledge, although Marx's is not as radical as that of Mannheim or of some historicists or existentialists. Although Lenin accepts the "copy" theory of knowledge, Marx is generally believed to reject it, particularly in his glosses on Feuerbach. Yet, the "true" knowledge acquired by the individual in the classless society seems less the product of a scientific epistemology than the emergence of an implicit "copy" theory. In any event, those who accept the "copy" theory of knowledge ignore the contextual character of truth while relativists, as in the extreme case of Mannheim, deprive objectively communicable knowledge of its foundation.

The Contextual Nature of Knowing

The epistemological problem extends beyond the mere abstract fact that some ultimate act or state of knowing can never be encompassed within the framework of the known, that we can never get inside the head of the knower to perceive what he perceives. Even granting this, the identification of what is known is dependent upon the instrument through which knowledge is acquired and which cannot at the same time be known. Thus the visual perception of events is dependent upon the possession of an optic apparatus. Some advocates of physical realism regard perception as illusionary and angstrom waves as real. Yet the detection of angstrom waves depends upon a visual perceptual apparatus; their identification, on the other hand, depends upon the possession of a theory that defines "angstrom wave," that translates the counters of the apparatus into angstrom waves, and that justifies the assumption that different cadmium spectrum lines are virtually identical.

Yet visual perception is contextual in still a different sense. The identification of a color, for instance, has reference to a "normalized" or expected context. To say that an object is really blue, although it is perceived as green, might mean no more than that ordinary human beings would identify it as blue in natural sunlight without the intercession of a color filter. We also mean that when subjected to scientific apparatus, we would detect the proper number of angstrom waves that are associated with the color "blue." Thus we can never get outside of the framework which sets the limits for the operations that produce the states of knowing.

Modern neurophysiology rejects the naive Lockean point of view. Our sense impressions do not simply present to us the world we perceive. Our eyes, for instance, continually move as we observe external events. As a consequence, the sensory inputs to the brain do not present a stationary table as stationary; instead, the brain acting upon cues inherent in the sensory data must impose the stability that is perceived upon the shifting sensory inputs (but not upon the events; the table *is* stationary). We can account for perception only on the basis of a theory. In the language of communication theory, a complicated negative feedback operation produces stable perceptions from shifting sense impressions. On the other hand, if this complicated system for ingesting external information operates faultily, the organism's chances for survival are reduced unless it is placed in a protective environment, as is often done with individuals who are either temporarily or permanently deranged.

Sensory inputs would be valueless to the organism unless they were at the same time informational inputs. We must begin with knowledge, that is, with an ability to code incoming data, or we could never obtain it. Defects in knowledge can be rectified by negative feedback, but knowledge cannot be acquired by a *tabula rasa*. The physiological instinct of withdrawal of a hand from fire, for instance, can produce an association between the withdrawal of the hand and the reduction of the burning sensation only if these items function within a preexisting informational context. A number of mental processes are involved. There is an intuition that is largely preconscious. Fire and pain are intuited as connected. There is an identification. That glowing phenomenon is fire and it burns. There is the implicit understanding of a universal causal association. Fire burns flesh that is brought sufficiently close. Although such conclusions may be learned, they could not be learned unless there was a previously existing capability to acquire and to code information.

None of these mental operations is simple. We do not know how intuitions are produced, although we can speculate about this.[1] On the other hand we can construct formal theories based on our intuitions; these can then be confirmed or disconfirmed by evidence. The intuition itself, however, evanesces under our grasp.

Even identification is not a simple process. The items that are enumerated for purposes of identification depend upon recognition. Thus a dentist recognizes the dental work in the mouth of a deceased. Fingerprint patterns or voiceprints are asserted to be identical. In this way, we eventually identify a man as a particular man. On the other hand, is a robot a man? Suppose that it is capable of abstract thought and of moral behavior.

What are the points of identification that justify us in categorizing a particular observation? These points of identification are not matters of simple recognition. They may depend upon the relationship of the observations to a theoretical framework within which they receive interpretation. At least in the physical sciences, there are usually theoretical checks on whether identifications are plausible. Consider, for instance, the problems that I. Langmuir had with the Davis-Barnes experiment:

> Well, in the discussion, we questioned how, experimentally, you could examine the

1. See Kaplan, *Macropolitics,* p. 54.

whole spectrum; because each count, you see, takes a long time. There was a long series of alpha particle counts, that took two minutes at a time, and you had to do it ten or fifteen times and you had to adjust the voltage to a hundredth of a volt. If you have to go through steps of a hundredth of a volt each and to cover all the range from 330 up to 900 volts, you'd have quite a job. (Laughter) Well, they said that they didn't do it quite that way. They had found by some preliminary work that they did check with the Bohr orbit velocities so they knew where to look for them. They found them sometimes not exactly where they expected them but they explored around in that neighborhood and the result was that they got them with extraordinary precision. So high, in fact, that they were sure they'd be able to check the Rydberg constant more accurately than it can be done by studying the hydrogen spectrum, which is something like one in the 10^8. At any rate, they had no inhibitions at all as to the accuracy which could be obtained by this method especially since they were measuring these voltages within a hundredth of a volt. Anybody who looks at the setup would be a little doubtful about whether the electrons had velocities that were fixed and definite within $1/100$ of a volt because this is not exactly a homogeneous field. The distance was only about 5 mm in which they were moving along together.[2]

The properties at issue were defined by physical theory—not merely by simple observation—and the supposed identifications were unlikely according to a specific accepted theory, Bohr's theory of the hydrogen atom. Thus Langmuir was led by theoretical considerations to a rejection of observational identifications that had been made by Davis and Barnes and to an explanation of their mistake.

Worse difficulties arise in the case of social science identifications, for instance, in the claim that something is a case of imperialism, of capitalistic exploitation, of feudalism, or a product of a mirror image. Consider the circumstances of a Chamberlain who has to decide whether Hitler's moves in Europe were cases of minor aggression, of an attempt to upset the existing distribution of power in Europe, of an effort to impose German hegemony in Europe, of an attempt to rectify an unjust treaty, of a desire to include ethnic Germans within the third Reich, or of injured national pride. The relevant theories are poor,

2. I. Langmuir, *Pathological Science,* edited and transcribed by R. N. Hall, General Electric, *Technical Information Series,* report no. 68-C-035 (Schenectady, New York: General Electric Research and Development Center, April 1968), pp. 2, 3.

THE CONTEXTUAL NATURE OF KNOWING

the concepts poorly defined within them, the criteria for identification far from obvious, and disagreement on usage great.

Intuitions

Intuitions provide knowledge—sometimes better and more useful knowledge than is provided by scientific method. We do not, for instance, know how to build a computer capable of the complex recognition patterns that the human mind is capable of. The experienced craftsman who observes a metal alloy under conditions of flame can often specify the components of the alloy to a precision not yet obtainable by scientific method except through the most expensive and time-consuming methods, and sometimes not even then. Tea and wine tasters perform their work with a subtlety that mechanical contrivances cannot yet achieve. The rules for acquiring such knowledge often cannot be transmitted, although identifications can be made and, in some cases, confirmed: for instance, that a particular tea is a sample of such and such a district, of such and such a vintage year. To the question, "What is this wine?" the answer, "Chablis, year 1957, *grand cru,* and so forth," is a valid information-providing answer. It is an answer for the "what" type of question. It is not an explanation in the "why" sense. (Intuitions may form the basis for theories also. After conception, theories are formulated and confirmed or falsified by the methods of science.)

Much of social science rests upon identifications that are at least partly incommunicable, at least in the present state of knowledge, and that depend upon experience and skill. Thus, it is absurd to believe that the neophyte interprets historical evidence, or that he even identifies historical entities, as does the learned scholar and that these differences can be fully identified and coded. We cannot yet "train" computers to make any except the simplest identifications. Although the efforts by historians and social scientists (a subject that will be returned to in the next chapter) to code their materials preparatory to quantitative analysis are commendable, they risk leaving out of account essential elements that cannot be quantified and others that they are unable to specify. This risk will be small in many cases; in others, and likely with respect to the larger and more important questions, it will likely be most significant. Thus, if this argument is correct, there will be for this reason significant qualitative—and even to some extent, nonscientific—elements in social science identifications.

The common-language philosophers misjudge the problem of identification and of intuition and mislead us into sterile pathways. John von Neumann speculated that the preconscious language of intuition employs a code qualitatively different from that of conscious language—a code that is more reliable but less precise. Whether this is true or not, we do not know what the preconscious code is. Therefore, explorations of common language cannot be known to assist us in learning about intuitions. On the other hand, extensive investigations in ordinary language divert us in large part from the investigation of the stipulative languages in which scientific propositions or theories are formulated. Although some linguistic analysis is necessary, it is merely a tool, not an end in itself.

The "Truth" Value of Theories

Definitions are conventional in the sense that the association of a word or of a sound with an external phenomenon is a matter of convention. Definitions may be chosen for convenience or because particular sets of definitions are more useful in exploring particular problems than other sets of definitions. Yet the identifications or definitions will not be useful unless there is really something in the world for which they serve as a referent.

Definitions and identifications have greatest utility within the framework of a theory. Theories have also come under attack as mere conveniences or as conventional paradigms. Although the choice of a theory is dependent upon the problem one wants to solve, it would be difficult to believe in the objectivity of knowledge if the various theories did not apply to a knowable external world. Although it is possible to live one's ordinary life on earth under the assumption that time is absolute, it is difficult to believe that Einsteinian theory is a mere convenience of the physicists for their problems. We will shortly explain the sense in which relativity theory invalidates the ordinary commonsense concept of absolute time. As a preliminary, we will attempt to deal with the claim that theories are mere conveniences or paradigms as evidenced by the fact that new paradigms are proposed by younger rather than older scientists. (Even this claim, of course, is a proposition which, if true, would invalidate itself; that is, it implies a claim that it is true regardless of the purpose or convenience of the proposer.)

Even if it is true, for instance, that new theories tend to be accepted by young scientists and to be rejected by old scientists, there are explanations for this that are more plausible than is the assumption that theories are merely conveniences. In the first place, older scientists have built their reputations on the theories they have developed, accepted, and based their work upon. Thus it is plausible that they would resist new theoretical formulations. In the second place, older scientists are probably less flexible mentally and probably more attuned to perceiving experimental results that accord with accepted theories.

Langmuir, in his discussion of pathological science, showed that many scientists, even some who were initially skeptical, accepted the Davis-Barnes effect, N-rays, mitogenetic rays, and the Allison effect, even though these were not genuine. How much easier it is not to perceive experimental results that are genuinely there when these do not accord with expectations. In the third place, scientists, particularly theoretical scientists, seem by psychological inclination to be disposed to reject established beliefs. The incentives for this to operate upon young scientists would seem greater than upon older scientists, who have become members of the scientific establishment. In the fourth place, it is easier for a young scientist to establish his reputation by means of a theoretical innovation than by building upon the work of an established figure. All these considerations would make it more likely that young, rather than old, scientists would be innovators. These hypotheses are objective in the "normal" philosophy of science sense. The "paradigm" argument therefore assumes the view it argues against, thus contradicting itself, or it lacks probative value. In any event, the observations to which it refers can be better explained by a view of science based on law.

New theories are usually more inclusive than discarded theories; they usually provide for more coherence in scientific phenomena—at least coherence with respect to results that can still be preserved against attack—and they usually provide more power-ful explanations and contain fewer ad hoc hypotheses. In addition, new theories often explain why the old theories are wrong or incomplete, or why they give approximations as good as they do where they do work. For instance, relativity theory explains, as Newtonian mechanics does not, the shift of light around an intermediary body. In addition, however, relativity theory explains why Newtonian mechanics gives as good an approximation as it does where it does work. According to the use of the Lorentz contraction in relativity theory, time slows for a system as it moves away from another system when the time of one is given by the "clock" of the other. However, within solar distances, for instance, the effects are so small—a traveler to the moon ages one second or so less than he would have aged had he remained on earth—that we understand why people are able to use the Newtonian equations with little difficulty for the problems they attempt to solve with them. Thus, it is not simply the case that relativity theory sets itself different problems from those of Newtonian mechanics; it explains the same problems as those of Newtonian mechanics better and at the same time indicates why the Newtonian system worked as well as it did. The fact that it does these things increases the power of Einsteinian relativity theory. Thus one can no longer speak of Newtonian mechanics as true, even with respect to the problems to which it addressed itself and which it solved reasonably well, but can only speak of it as providing a reasonable approximation within solar distances for some problems. If relativity theory is displaced by another theory, that theory likely will explain better the same phenomena that relativity theory explains; it likely will explain why relativity theory does as well as it does; or it will invalidate relativity theory except as a method for obtaining approximations in that case in which the new theory's domain of explanatory power is smaller than that of relativity theory. Moreover, its domain will not become smaller unless experimental results occur which invalidate relativity theory within the larger domain.

If we state that theories are discarded for new theories when the weight of evidence goes against the old theories, we are not talking merely about the quantity of evidence, for no one really knows how to measure these quantities in any significant sense. The evidence that goes against an old theory must also be qualitative; it must establish the case that the old theory no longer offers a good explanation, that is, that the old laws are not true. The evidence that goes against the theory must be evidence that disconfirms one of its central or most general principles. In this sense, a single replicated negative instance may invalidate a theory, whereas in other cases cumulative additions of evidence may be thought to involve measurement error or petty matters that will be explained or tidied up later. For instance, a demonstration that the gravitational constant is weakening over time would be sufficient to invalidate Einstein's formulation of the general theory of relativity. On the other hand, a great mass of experimental evidence not fully consistent with the most general principles of relativity theory does not produce a serious challenge to Einstein's formulation of it.

When one theory replaces another, it is usually because the previous theory has been shown not to offer a genuine explanation. Thus, although the domain of a new theory may be smaller than the previously accepted domain of the old theory, its new domain is larger than the now (often) zero domain of the old theory. The explanatory domain of spiritualism was extremely broad, but it is now believed by most people to explain nothing. Sometimes the questions and subject matters posed by newer theories are different from those of older ones, at least in part. But in this case the old answers are not so much improved upon as bypassed. And sometimes older theories are incorrectly believed to have been falsified.

The history of physical science nonetheless does appear to provide a progression, if not a simple one. Although the seventeenth-century view that all science would be explained according to one coherent theory has been discarded, science is cumulative in the following sense: its range of explanatory power —apart from that of any single scientific theory— increases over that of the past; the number of discoveries per unit of time increases; control over physical change increases over time; control over biology increases over time; the interconnection between ranges of explanation as in biophysics, even if there is no common theory, increases over time. Nonetheless there is nothing in scientific method that requires the seventeenth-century view of a single theory encompassing all of life, let alone even all of its physical aspects. The theories that were discarded for the most part failed to explain observed experimental evidence, required large numbers of ad hoc explanatory devices, and ceased to provide a base from which further useful work, either experimental or theoretical, could be carried forward.

Explanations and Theories

"Poison kills" is a truistic explanation of an apparent "why" type (as is "power corrupts"), but a weak and unreliable one. "Poison deprives the blood of oxygen" is a better explanation that begins to answer "why" type questions. "Poison deprives the blood of oxygen, leading to cellular brain damage, leading to non-transmission of neural messages across synapses, leading to the cessation of breathing and the stoppage of the heart, in the absence of which life is not possible" is still a much better explanation of the "why" type. If a person is given poison and then given an antidote that prevents the poison from depriving the blood of oxygen, the second explanation provides us with knowledge of why the generalization did not apply to the particular case. The third explanation is better yet, for it enables us to explain cases of interference at many points in the process. For instance, we might find an antidote that does not prevent the blood from being deprived of oxygen but that does prevent cellular brain damage. Moreover, the explanation is more satisfying even in the absence of this, for it provides an explanation in the context of the operation of the human physiological system, that is, within terms of boundary conditions.

This latter explanatory framework both explains how and why poison works and justifies the designation of particular agents as poisons. Properly expressed, it does so in a universalistic nomological-deductive form in which laws connect the explanandum events with the particular conditions cited in the explanans.[3]

3. See Carl G. Hempel, "Explanation in Science and in History," in Robert G. Colodny, editor, *Frontiers of Science and Philosophy* (Pittsburgh: University of Pittsburgh Press, 1962), pp. 9–15, for an explanation of nomological-deductive methods.

Theories in the strict sense involve laws, theorems, deduced conclusions, the specification of boundary conditions, and the specification of the evidence that will confirm or falsify the theory. Not all the terms or concepts used in theories can be defined in descriptive language, although boundary conditions and confirming or disconfirming evidence must be specified in descriptive language. Explanations in the strict sense are provided by theories. Explanation sketches —a subject that will be returned to later in this chapter—provide explanations in a looser sense.

Laws are not merely conditional universal statements, however. A law will sustain counterfactual and subjunctive conditional statements. Thus, for instance, the counterfactual subjunctive assertion that a rocket would have fallen except for its possession of an adequate and functioning propellant device can be derived from the laws of gravitation, which therefore provide a "why" type answer to the question "Why did not the rocket fall?" One can answer, "It would have fallen except for the propellant device." Statements such as "All the apples in this basket are red" sustain universal conditional statements such as "If X is an apple in this basket, it is red" but do not answer counterfactual subjunctive conditional questions such as "If X is an apple and is in the basket and is not red, why is this so?" Such statements therefore are not laws and do not explain in the "why" sense.

We will shortly consider an objection by Michael Scriven to this mode of analysis. Before doing so, it is useful to distinguish lawlike sentences from laws and disposition statements from both. A lawlike sentence, unlike completely general laws, includes mention of particular objects. Thus, for instance, Kepler's laws, as originally conceived, apply only to the motions of solar planets. Such lawlike statements, however, can often be subsumed under completely general laws; Kepler's laws, for instance, can be subsumed under Newton's laws of gravitation and motion. Where this cannot be done, dispositional sentences can be formulated for purposes of explanation.[4] Such sentences state the sufficient conditions for the presence of a disposition, for instance, for a metal to have great tensile strength or for a man to behave irrationally. These are not merely definitional, for it is a factual or synthetic matter that when the sufficient conditions for a disposition are present, all necessary conditions

4. See Carl G. Hempel, *Aspects of Scientific Explanation and Other Essays in the Philosophy of Science* (New York: The Free Press of Glencoe, 1965), pp. 457ff, for a discussion of lawlike sentences and dispositional sentences. For the original formulation of reduction sentences, see Rudolf Carnap, "Testability and Meaning," *Philosophy of Science* 3:419–71 (1936) and 4:1–40 (1937). The article by Professor Hempel has a more complete discussion of nomological-deductive methods than the one cited in the previous note.

will be present. This is related to attempts to explain history through motivation, for dispositional sentences are lawful; thus motivations imply nomological laws in Hempel's sense.[5]

Dray, for instance, attempts to employ a principle of action that is largely based upon a concept of rationality to explain historical behavior.[6] The concept of rationality, however, is a difficult one; it is not clear that there is any single valid concept applicable to all situations or different concepts that are productive of univocal solutions in all particular situations.[7] The concept of rationality is useful in explanations only if it can be shown independently

5. See Morton A. Kaplan, "Problems of Theory Building and Theory Confirmation in International Politics," in Klaus E. Knorr and Sidney Verba, editors, *The International System* (Princeton: Princeton University Press, 1961), pp. 16–17, for a discussion of the fact that international systems models are predictive when stated boundary conditions hold, that is, that defined rational behavior is dependent on specified empirical conditions.

6. William Dray, "The Historical Explanation of Actions Reconsidered," in Sidney Hook, editor, *Philosophy and History* (New York: New York University Press, 1963), pp. 105ff.

7. See Morton A. Kaplan, "A Note on Game Theory and Bargaining," in Kaplan, editor, *New Approaches to International Relations* (New York: St. Martin's Press, 1968), pp. 494–506.

that an agent is (or likely is) rational in the given sense. If this can be done or attempted, explanations employing rationality or reasons as elements have the appropriate deductive form. Thus we cannot infer that Bismarck, for instance, likely intended X, which he achieved, unless it can be shown in particular that X was in some sense an appropriate objective for Bismarck and that Bismarck was rational in the specified sense. The attempt to use the concept of rationality in explanations, as Dray does, apart from such demonstrations, is ineffectual. Dray has avoided the deductive form in favor of a "principle of action" of the form "When in a situation of type C, the thing to do is X," only by ignoring essential elements of explanation. It may indeed be the case that X is the thing to do in situation C, but not for Bismarck, or that Bismarck was not rational in the assumed sense and intended Y rather than X. One must be able to show that Bismarck accepted X as a reasonable objective and that he was capable of proceeding and did proceed "rationally" to obtain it. If one can do this, however, one has an explanation in deductive form that is based on a law.

An Objection to This Account of Explanation
The use of laws in explanations, as formulated by Carl G. Hempel and Karl Popper, has been attacked by a number of scholars, including, most powerfully,

Michael Scriven. To avoid misinterpretation, Scriven's argument is quoted at length:

> First then, I wish to dispose of two arguments sometimes felt to establish the absolute necessity for supposing laws of the Hempelian kind to underlie our explanations. The occupational hazard for any such argument was brought out earlier: it is likely to be self-defeating if it becomes too general, since it then obliterates the distinction between explanations and, e.g., descriptions. In any sense in which laws underlie descriptions, they do not constitute part of a logical analysis of explanations as a distinct category of discourse. Take the view that laws underlie ("are involved in") explanations because any working language presupposes regularities (since communication requires constancies of meanings, and these require constancies of reference, i.e., regularities in the world). This does not show that laws are involved in explanations in any way they are not involved in particular statements, and it is certainly of the greatest irrelevance to tell a historian that his statements about the number of pottery shards he has discovered at the Acropolis excavations "really" involve laws (e.g., about the continued existence of something which can be called "the Acropolis") and would be "more completely formulated" if these were explicitly stated. This is an entirely mislead-

ing sense of "involves," a trivial, irrelevant sense, and if this is the only sense in which explanations involve laws we can ignore it. In certain highly abnormal contexts (e.g., where our sight begins to fail us but we haven't yet realized it), some of these regularity-presuppositions of ordinary descriptive talk may be at issue and have to be uncovered. But in virtually every ordinary case (and necessarily, since language could otherwise never operate effectively for communication) both description and explanation are complete without laws and cannot be made *more* complete by giving the presupposed "laws" (they not only would be redundant, but cannot be formulated, and are unnecessary either for verification purposes or for understanding). The difference between them is the element of understanding, of which the one has, of its nature, to be the bearer.

Look now at the supposedly Humean argument, which at least avoids the possibility of a simple *reductio ad absurdum* move such as we have just employed. At best, it only applies to causal explanations and hence not to all historical explanations. But it does *not* apply to all descriptive statements and this saves it from the death by excess. What can it mean to offer something, C, as the cause of something else, E? That C is a cause of E as well as being an event of a certain describable kind cannot be dis-

AN OBJECTION TO THIS ACCOUNT OF EXPLANATION

covered by examining C *alone*. It appears to be an inference of a more complicated kind from C's *relation* to other events, including E; in fact, it is argued, the causal assertion can only mean that C's are *constantly conjoined* with E's. Here is the regularity, law, or universal hypothesis, which is supposed to be involved in the causal assertion. It is part of the meaning of "cause." I think that an oversight on the part of Hume and, so far as I can see, his successors (certainly Russell and Hempel), vitiates this argument entirely. (But it may well be that a more serious one vitiates this criticism!) I shall argue that the only sense in which they are correct is one which involves an absurd sense of "law."

Their argument is strongest at the general level, for as we take specific uses of "cause" we find their analysis of this term to be faulty. Assume that part of their analysis to be correct; then the form of their argument goes thus: "You say that C caused E, but that you do not think any general causal law is involved. But surely you cannot mean that C caused E just on *this* occasion, and that something *exactly like* C *would not* bring about something exactly like E on another occasion. If you did mean this, what is it about this occasion that entitles you to distinguish the two occasions, to say that *here alone* C causes E? Whatever it is, it should be included in the description of C, since it is a causally relevant condition; and then you will no longer have any grounds for rejecting the general law asserting that C's (as now described) always produce E's."

To this, one can reply very directly: "It is not clear what can be meant by *exactly like.* If it means 'alike in all features I can at the moment describe,' then I can certainly reject the generalization, for there may well be features to this C which are of great causal importance, and which I have taken into account in forming my judgment that C produced E, but which I may not be very good at formulating exactly—just as the experienced helmsman can with extreme reliability identify the cause of a yacht's defeat as sailing too close to the wind, but be quite unable to formulate a general law of which this case could be shown to be an instance. There is no necessary connection between reliability in identifying causes and reliability in formulating laws; and as a historian, one need have no interest in, and no faith in the future of, the search for gross laws of human behavior.

"On the other hand, perhaps by 'exactly like' you meant 'alike in every respect, presently describable or not.' Then I reject the generalization on the grounds that it has no generality. For the assertion that the explanation of the occurrence of the scientific revolution in Western rather than Eastern Europe was the devastation of the Eastern

Empire by the barbarians coupled with the genius of Galileo, cannot be generalized in such a way as to say the generalization has ever been found to be true before or since. So my (justifiable) confidence in the explanation has nothing to do with any belief in this 'generalization.' "

There are two possible defenses here. First it might be said that, even if the explanation's strength cannot be increased by production of such a law—hitherto unconfirmed—yet the explanation logically requires one to assert such a law. Unfortunately, the argument is wrong not only pragmatically but logically; for even if a belief in some law is required for the assertion that C causes E, it need not be a law that C's cause E's. It may be a law in which time occurs; so that the effect said to be produced by C's varies with time, ranging from E's (at this particular time) to F's (at a later time) to G's etc. Such a law would perfectly support prediction and causation and could be inferred from available data; it is in fact a good model for development laws about the changing responses of an individual as he learns from experience. If any laws are found in history, they may well be of this kind; and there is therefore no contradiction at all between saying that C caused E (now) and denying that C's cause E's in general, i.e., that any Hempelian kind of law is involved. The laws that psychologists seek in learning studies are not of this kind. They *are* intended to have multiple instances—all organisms, all mammals, all white rats, all white rats of a certain strain. The narrowing down can be continued without loss of interest, though the kind of interest comes nearer to the interest of the historian than the psychologist, up to the point where we have a law about the behavior of a single individual. And some of these can have a fully causal form without in any way involving the assertion that more than one similar action will or *could* be covered. If you like, we can still talk of a generalization here, but it is one in which the instances are different. So there is no need for the kind of generalization that Hempel defines as a "universal hypothesis" at all, neither a practical nor a logical need.

One cannot include the time in the description of C because C is, in Hempel's words, "a . . . kind of event," and two events cannot be said to be of a different *kind* simply because one occurs later than another. (A similar distinction could be made in terms of space; and the result of accepting them would be the view that each event defines a kind of event, i.e., the laws *necessarily* have generality in the sense that it is *logically possible* for them to apply to more than one event. Hence for "kind of event" to make sense it cannot include reference to spacetime location as such.) It is true that the above discussion rules out Hempelian laws by showing that a more general kind meets Hume's requirement. But the time-dependent laws also ruin the point of Hume's argument, since we clearly can *not* give them and clearly *do* have causal judgments that are beyond reasonable doubt (think of the ink-stain example). The challenge to justify such judgments hence does not require the *giving of kinds* of event C and E which are here instantiated and in general related; and the remaining Humean requirement—that there *be* such laws—can certainly not be disproved, but has no effect on the procedure of identifying and verifying causal claims.

Perhaps one still feels that an element of universality remains. Surely to say C caused E *logically* commits one to the view that anything identical to C in every respect *including the time* will produce something similarly identical to E. Here indeed we reach agreement—but not significance. For it is *logically impossible* that there could be more than one thing satisfying this requirement, and to talk of a generalization which cannot possibly have more than one instance is really to abuse the concept. A particularly unattractive feature of this piece of logical legerdemain is that it converts the most highly individual statement into a generalization; for to say "Lord Haldane suggested to the Coal Commission that the spirit of

devoted service characteristic of the professional military services would be an excel-
lent ideal for the state-owned civilian enter-
prises" is to say that Lord Haldane and
everyone exactly identical to him suggested
. . . i.e., to produce a "generalization" or
"law" or "universal hypothesis" in the sense
used above. This is clearly an entirely trivial
manoeuvre. A generalization must have
more than one possible instance; a particular
statement is no less particular because it applies to "everything" logically identical to
its subject.[8]

A Rebuttal

Scriven treats scientific laws as if they were independent of context. He also treats electrons and people
as if identity were a simple matter in both cases. The
fact that scientific laws in physics do not talk about
the internal states of electrons, whereas laws of psychology, should we ever discover these, would necessarily include psychic states, seems to escape his attention. Yet we cannot make the latter sort of
identification in the absence of a scientific theory.

It is not true, for instance, that scientific laws really

8. Michael Scriven, "Truisms as the Grounds for Historical Explanations," in Patrick Gardiner, editor, *Theories of History* (Glencoe, Illinois: The Free Press, 1959;
London: Allen and Unwin, 1960); reprinted by permission of the publishers.

state that all C's are constantly conjoined with E's. In the first place, a law is a statement about properties of entities and not about entities directly. Moreover, unless statements such as those offered by Scriven are understood as elliptical, they would imply that the asserted relationships were independent of context, that is, of boundary conditions. The laws of motion, for instance, depend upon the existence of a vacuum. Many such parameters can be stated, but we can never know that all have been. We can take account of the known factors that interfere with direct predictions from a law and engineer the example for them. We can never exclude the possibility that some unknown factor will falsify a statement, although, as our range of knowledge increases, the generality of our system of assertions also increases and our confidence that the asserted laws are in fact laws increases.

Scriven speaks as if learning theory were genuinely time dependent, in the sense that time was the essential difference that made an identical stimulus produce different behavior. This is not so, for the relevant difference is the difference in the informational state of the organism. We know that human behavior is information dependent. Although we are able to make statements about behavior related to information that are largely pragmatic, that is, statements induced from limited experience rather than derived from theory, they are on the order of the statement that "Poison kills." Their explanatory power is extremely limited and would be increased greatly by being comprehended within the framework of a behavioral theory that had information as one of its elements, in the same way as our statements concerning the effects of poison are increased in explanatory power as we are able to include them within the framework of an appropriate general physiological theory embodying laws or dispositional sentences.

The interesting thing about the process of explanation is that, contrary to Scriven's contention, increased specification does not make for mere descriptive particularization but instead occurs within the framework of a universal theory of great explanatory power. These are not cases of single instances; they are genuine generalizations, as I indicate below. Even the identifications or "what" elements are relevant primarily within their framework.

Although little in history can be raised to this level of power, at least on the basis of present-day social science, and although some reasonable degree of useful information is provided by less powerful techniques, even these techniques are by implication universalizations. Thus "Poison kills" is a universal statement, although, because of the failure to specify boundary conditions, it is of an extremely low order of power and not a law. One does not improve it by greater particularization, as in Scriven's example concerning Lord Haldane, but instead by greater articulation. If we say that Lord X was poisoned but did not die, an explanation of this implies the framework of an appropriate physiological theory employing universal laws. The boundary conditions of such theories can never be known to have been completely stated, but even descriptions can never be completely stated. Particular statements, such as that concerning Lord Haldane, involve explanations from diverse perspectives. The ways in which such constraints are applied are discussed in several places in this book, including later in this chapter; Scriven, however, confuses the entire issue by the type of singular explanation he offers. Indeed, Scriven either implicitly derives his assertions of cause from universal generalizations or he is making a most mysterious claim to be able to perceive causes.[9]

9. Scriven argues that if one knocks over an open ink bottle, he knows that an ink stain will occur on the rug but that this cannot be deduced from any theory. Hempel has appropriately pointed out that the occurrence of the blot can be deduced from relevant physical laws and a statement of such conditions as the relation of the open bottle to the rug. As Hempel correctly states, the shape of the stain cannot be deduced, at least by current methods, from such information. However, he doubts that Scriven "knows" the cause of this singular property or that he can relate it in any publicly communicable fashion to another person.

Scriven adverts to a number of historical generalizations, such as "Power corrupts," that he offers as useful truisms that do not involve causal generalizations. The poor state of historical writing misleads him. These so-called truisms have little positive explanatory power and may even be harmful to understanding. Statements that pretend to be true about everything are likely either to be true about almost nothing or to be trivial. "Lack of power corrupts" is also true and is a much more powerful negative statement than "Poison does not kill"; Scriven's truism does not tell us anything about the type of system within which power corrupts or within which lack of power corrupts. This lack of theoretical articulation, and the consequent lack of an effort to strive for laws, is destructive of the power of historical understanding, for an explicit awareness of implied laws is even more necessary in history, where it is more difficult to determine relevant parameters, than in the physical sciences where the necessity of articulating boundary conditions is well known. Although "Poison does not kill" is a true statement—the effects of poison are dependent on the kind of poison and its strength as well as on the physiological system in which it is introduced, its condition, and other circumstances—in practice it vitiates the utility of "Poison kills" less than "Lack of power corrupts" vitiates the utility of "Power corrupts."

A REBUTTAL

If, however, we attempt to deal with a system of articulated and interconnected relations, as is true of any good theory; if we attempt to state boundary conditions and relevant evidence; then the qualifications that are necessary to produce the deduction are informative, meaningful, and explanatory. They do not reduce the range of application to a particular case but instead draw the relevant properties within an articulated and universal web. For instance, with respect to the types of international theories—really theory sketches—that I deal with, a "balance of power" theory explains why the results predicted by the theory were produced for different reasons in classical Greece, why the behavior predicted by the theory did not occur after 1870 in Europe, and why in the cases of the Greek-Macedonian system and the Chinese warlord system, the proper explanation of the roll-up of the system by a peripheral power is produced by the theory rather than by Toynbee's hypothesis.[10] Because we have a theory sketch rather than a theory, "explanation" should be understood in a loose sense. Because boundary conditions are not completely stated, because the criteria for confirming or falsifying evidence are loose, and because the properties of the system are not known to be additive, tests of such "theories" are not possible in a strict sense.

10. See Kaplan, *Macropolitics,* pp. 209ff.

However, because an effort is made to articulate universal statements in a partial deductive chain and because some boundary conditions and some criteria for evidence are specified, the effort comes closer to science and to explanations than more traditional approaches.

Problems in Theory Building and Explanation

The problem of historical explanations and their relationship to universal statements, however, is not disposed of. Scriven's critique of Hempel on the subject of particularization is misguided but does respond to a real problem. However, he has not found the core of the problem and thus misperceives it. The social world is more obdurate to the development of theory than is the world of science, although even there similar problems occur.

The advance of theory in physical science, since Galileo, has depended in important ways upon a choice of problems permitting simple laboratory experiments that can be isolated from contaminating influences and comparatively simple mathematical modeling. Neither condition appears to hold for the social sciences where outside influences cannot be eliminated and where they are apparently not merely additive.

Unlike the Greeks, who sought solutions for perfect motions, such as circles, Galileo chose a much simpler problem. There is, for instance, a single general formula according to which all two-body problems can be solved, given their starting positions. Attempts to solve interaction problems involving a large number of bodies require the iterated application of the formula for the two-body problem. This is an important qualification, for attempts to solve the multibody problem involve the very same simplifying assumptions concerning system parameters as in the two-body problem—that is, for instance, frictionless motion—but nonetheless become increasingly particularized in the sense that the universal formula requires an iterated engineering solution. Therefore, apart from problems of measurement error or of interaction between measurer and measured object, the more complicated the problem becomes, the closer we get to the particularities of the real world than to the laws most characteristic of theoretical physical science. Nonetheless, the particularized engineering solution for the problem is impossible in the absence of a law.

An important second factor also comes into play. In the physical sciences the concept of equality in laws embodying mechanical equilibria is meaningful because there are independent measures for the variables and genuine equalities between them. When we turn to examples of homeostatic equilibria—and all social or political "equilibria" are variations of the homeostatic variety—we no longer have independent measures or genuine equalities. Therefore, the implication of equality in "equilibrium" is not genuinely related to governing laws. Hence the concept of equilibrium is not in this case an explanatory device with respect to "why" questions but is merely a categorizing device that tells us something about "what" we are dealing with. Thus, with respect to social or political systems, the universe must be divided into types of systems. Even in the physical sciences, however, explanations, except at the truistic or tautological level, apply only to the properly designated type of system. Precision of formulation is such, however, in the sciences that a cautionary notice to this effect is superfluous.

In the social sciences self-consciousness with respect to system differentiation is particularly important. We do not have, for instance, good measures for demands and supports considered independently let alone any method for equating them or for measuring system efficiency in processing them. The concept of equality is thus tautological in this case and essentially meaningless. We might get indicators of at least temporary validity concerning system strains; these are hardly likely to hold good for different kinds of systems or even for the same system over time. Primarily, we will have to depend on models of how particular kinds of systems operate, what kinds of roles are performed, and why individuals are motivated to perform adequately roles in some subsystems and not in others when parameter changes produce subsystem disequilibrium. If we have good theory sketches of why a type of subsystem performs in given ways, we will then have partial explanations of why particular kinds of parameter disturbances will produce particular kinds of responses and of whether those responses are likely to dampen or to exacerbate the disturbances. These partial explanations will involve centrally those characteristics of a system that distinguish it from others. Thus, for instance, Communist and authoritarian regimes function differently against both country and city guerrilla disturbances. These differences between Communist and authoritarian regimes can be understood in large part in terms of differences between them — for instance, control mechanisms, ideology, and so forth. For this reason comparative method rather than general theory is essential. The things that are true of all political systems are truistic in the bad sense of the term. We do not deal here merely with a question of comparative boundary conditions that affect the operations of a political system (although that problem also constitutes an argument for comparative method). More important, comparative method, in this case, draws attention to basic differences in the systems themselves and in the theory sketches that are used to explain them.

Universals and Particulars:
The Real and the Nominal

Universal laws fail to account entirely for historical events. No description can exhaust reality and no single theory or theory sketch can fully account for it. The first consideration takes us into the old debate between nominalists and realists, that is, between particularists and universalists.

In accord with the Peircean analysis, I regard that debate as misleading. According to the pragmaticist theory of knowledge, no series of experiments can exhaust the attributes of particular objects of experience. And no description can ever exhaust the particularities of an entity. Neither can any theory exhaust the existential world. Even in the simpler aspects of the physical sciences, for instance, in Newton's laws of motion, simplifying assumptions are made that real conditions only approximate. Finer and finer approximations can be made. These are often not very important from the standpoint of the experimenter, although there are some critical exceptions to this. The fact that he can usually isolate his variables from a contaminating environment means that he can predict what will occur within the framework of a single theory. Whether individual electrons, or other elementary particles, are really exactly alike is not a problem even for the experimenter in the realm of microphysics where the interaction between the observer and the observed phenomena cannot be completely damped.

The experimenter identifies the experimental situations as one encompassed by a theory which explains the behavior within it. This is not arbitrary, however, as the relevant antecedent conditions have been stated. We treat the experimental situation as if the theory exhausted its meaning or as if it came reasonably close to doing so. The closer the fit between theory and event, the more satisfied we are with the theory. We are less satisfied with seemingly contradictory schemas: for instance, that theoretical models treating light as if it consisted of waves are employed in certain kinds of situations and that in others theoretical models treating light as if it consisted of particles are employed. We would believe that our explanations for the phenomenon of light are more truly explanatory if we had a single theoretical schema that explained why light behaved as if it were a particle in a particular experimental environment and why it behaved as if it were a wave in other environments. In fact, quantum theory, which does not employ a "picture language," does this. The better a theory, the more it will comprehend a wide range of phenomena within a single explanatory framework that accounts for the differences of behavior under differing conditions, as is true of physical theory in the case of superconductivity.

In the social and historical sciences, a single theoretical sketch will only rarely, if at all, encompass the various aspects of the social and political world. This means that the approximations between our models or theories and the phenomena to be explained will almost always have much more in the way of residue than in the case of the physical sciences. Moreover, different theories will explain different aspects of the same situation or problem. Therefore the particularities of events will almost always be more important in the social and political sciences than in the physical sciences. This is not a matter of principle, however, although the reasons that will be given seem compelling.

The distinctions between the two realms are by no means absolute, for there are some aspects of social and political science to which reasonable "theoretical" approximations can be made, and there are some aspects of the physical sciences where engineering applications of theory involve a welter of particularities. If, for instance, Truman wanted to know whether American fission bombs would destroy Japanese cities, he had to know whether these bombs would be properly constructed and placed on the bombers, whether the bombers would reach their target, and whether the bombardiers would release them, as well as whether the bombs would work. No single theory sketch encompasses this range of questions, and we do not know how to construct theories that would do so. Nonetheless, explanatory frameworks in the social and physical sciences run the risk of merely skimming the surface of the particularity to be explained; and this is especially true the closer we come to the level of microevents.

Historical Explanation and
Diversity of Framework

When we try to explain why President John F. Kennedy acted the way he did in the Cuban missile crisis, we can offer explanations from a wide variety of frameworks based on different, but not contradictory, theoretical sketches. Each framework has only a limited bearing upon the event it is designed to explain. For instance, if we turn to psychological explanations, we suffer not merely from the fact that we are dealing with a "theory" standardized upon particular kinds of groups—for instance, possibly, sophomore girls in fashionable liberal arts colleges—but also from the fact that such explanations deal with tendencies, that is, with statistical probabilities, any of which may be contraindicated by particular items of information that may not be available to us. We may argue that Kennedy had such a kind of personality and that such and such a kind of person is likely to behave in such and such a kind of way in such and such a kind of situation and that he did. Yet these personality types are modal patterns that real personalities may only approximate.

The fit between theory and application in social and political history is by no means as good as that of macrophysics or even as that of microphysics. We can attempt explanations within the framework of alternative perspectives, for example, those of diplomatic alternatives, of strategic theory, of national politics, or organization theory, of intrigues within the executive network, and so forth, each one of which gives us a rather poorly tailored fit.

If a great many of the perspectives seem to limit choice to a few alternatives, or even to a single major alternative, then by a process of identification of the patterns with the situations, we regard the framework of choice as so restricted that the weight of the accumulated evidence seems to us to overcome the poorness of the fit of the individual theoretical sketches considered separately. The explanations reinforce each other rather than detract from each other.

Our explanatory power here is truistic in a sense, although not in the sense that Scriven suggests; our universal generalization is that the more restricted the choice pattern, the more likely an individual is to have made a particular choice, so that if he does something different from what we expect, that is precisely what requires to be explained. A truism such as "Power corrupts" does not provide us with even a restricted choice theorem.[11] There must be an accumulation of evidence sustaining the patterning for us to draw a conclusion.

Marion Levy has argued that the claim that a single comprehensive theory is unlikely in the realm of social microevents is based on a confusion. He says that we cannot know in advance that someone will not discover a simplification that will permit prediction; he points out that we cannot exclude the possibility of a theory that is general for the events of subatomic physics, for instance. His denials are reasonable, but the inferences he makes from them are not. The sheer number of the perspectives from which characteristics of social and political microevents can be explained makes for a powerful presumption against his view. Although it is possible that some ingenious invention will cut through what appears to be diversity of perspectives, the prospect that we will either achieve a fit even as good as that we sometimes achieve for macrosocial systems or that a single schema will incorporate all relevant perspectives seems exceptionally dubious.

Theories in the social and political sciences are

11. Other categories of historical explanation assert consistency of observation and theory (see the discussion of the Alsace-Lorraine case below) or a theorem of excluded choice (see the discussion of prudence and strategy in the next chapter).

much more likely to be found at the level of macro-events, for instance, at the level of comparative political theories with respect to national governments, or comparative theories with respect to international arenas, or with respect to family systems, and so forth. These can make powerful simplifying assumptions precisely because they deal with the macroframeworks within which microevents occur.

In his study of the Congress of Vienna, for instance, Harold Nicholson found that the shifting alignments on various issues depended on a number of accidental factors. In one case, for instance, a rude remark at dinner to the prince regent of England by the Czar's sister led to opposition on the part of the two countries on the next substantive issue at the Congress. However, the series of alignments satisfied criteria that can be derived from my "balance of power" theory sketch. A statesman who takes the system for granted could usefully focus his attention on micro-level constraints that predispose toward particular alignments. This could be a serious mistake if the system structure were itself unstable and sensitive to succeeding decisions. Similarly, attempts to use the United Nations Charter to outlaw force, attempts to extend the American system of alliances indefinitely, attempts to use the United Nations as primarily an instrument of American policy, and so forth, both mistook the system constraints of a loose bipolar system and were likely counterproductive in terms of the values intended for implementation. They overlooked the usefulness of uncommitted states in the system, confronted the United Nations with tasks it did not have the capability to perform and misused it when it proved incapable, and required, in the absence of other remedies, a degree of restraint from other states that was inconsistent with their vital security and interests.

Although the most important question in the world to John Smith and Susie Jones may be whether they will marry or to President Nixon how the Russians will respond to a particular move, we will do much better with events of this kind when we use the principle of restricted choice (for instance, the strategic nuclear and local nonnuclear restraints on Brezhnev's policy options) than when we employ global theories. On the other hand, although the following matters have less immediate importance to young people looking forward to marriage or to presidents looking toward immediate decisions, we can use theory sketches, for instance, to study the conditions under which nuclear families are likely to arise and the changes in external conditions that are likely to make for changes in the behavior of nuclear families. We can use theory sketches to study the differences between "balance of power" international systems and bipolar systems and the conditions under which bipolar systems are likely, for instance, to be transformed in any of several ways and the impact this may possibly have upon the framework of international law, upon the incidence of war, or the ways in which wars are conducted. Our predictions from any one of these frameworks with respect to a microevent can be given only low confidence except in the case, which is rare, where a single framework dominates the event.

The fit between a theoretical sketch and an existential particularity is not usually good; nor is a particular theoretical sketch often sufficiently dominant, in the absence of other reinforcing frameworks, to restrict choice sufficiently for a good prediction. Nonetheless the use of several relevant theoretical sketches will likely aid us in understanding and explaining why choices are restricted.

No sensible person would want the president of the United States to derive national policy either from macrostrategic theory or from more particular computer simulations based on such theories; nonetheless a president of the United States unable to understand the restrictions placed upon his possible decisions by correct strategic choice and analysis is a president who lacks an essential tool for the decision-making process. No one would desire the president of the United States to derive his policy toward the United Nations from a loose bipolar international systems model; but a president of the United States who is unable to understand the macrorelations of entities in an international system is a president who may be sacrificing the future to the immediate exigencies of policy. One of the great failures in the analysis of international relations by historians stems from the fact that almost without exception they have no comprehension of the existence of a macroframework within which diplomatic behavior occurs. They thus often involve themselves in a morass of microevents that contribute some information concerning restricted choice patterns but often not nearly enough information.

When we deal with history, we deal not only with a subject that may be treated from many different perspectives, we deal with a subject where our universal explanatory frameworks are less like rather than more like the particularities they are designed to explain. We deal with a subject where within the independent explanatory frameworks, which we try to fit together into a pattern of restricted choice, the relationship is often so complicated that we cannot be sure how we derive conclusions. In deciding that choice is restricted in particular ways, we often have no good framework within which accurate weights can be assigned to particular perspectives or within which ad hoc relationships among them can be well articulated. Even the process of identification of a particular aspect of an event or of a series of events with a framework chosen to illuminate part of it is an identification based upon criteria that are subject to question. Often intuition is better than the articulated explanations we give to our choice patterns. But only some people have good intuitions and it is difficult to explain how to choose those with good intuitions or to determine the conditions under which their intuitions are good. Churchill's intuitions, for instance, were obviously quite appropriate to the situation of the late 1930s, but they were equally obviously much less good for the situation of the mid-1940s. Moreover, his intuitions were not uniformly good during the late 1930s or during the war but were better in some areas than in others. It is silly to think that the aphorisms he used to explain his intuitions genuinely explained much. They conveyed emotional tones and could not easily be used to distinguish his good intuitions from his poor intuitions. We unfortunately accept as explanations truisms that do almost anything but explain.

If, on the other hand, we have articulated theories or theory sketches, we can then identify properties of external world situations to which they are more or less applicable. We can look to see whether there are any specific variables which, when engineered into the theoretical sketch, give rise to a result other than the result predicted. For instance, that is how the explanation offered for the transformed behavior of the European international system after 1870 is engineered according to international systems theory.[12] Alliances are rigid, and the war of 1914 unlimited, contrary to the predictions of the model. In the theoretical sketch, however, policy is optimized for external conditions. The adjustment made is that for the state of French public opinion after 1870 and for the perturbations this introduces into the operations of the model. When this is done, one no longer expects alliances to be flexible and wars limited. Thus we have an explanation in the "why" sense.

The way in which a probabilistic theory can be used to explain a nonconforming event is illustrated by coin tossing. Over a large enough series of runs, we expect heads or tails to approach fifty percent of the outcomes. If this does not occur, we will examine the coin to see if it is so constructed that either heads or tails will likely come up more often than fifty percent of the time. If so, we have an explanation of the nonconforming event. In this case, however, we are dealing with a system of mechanical equilibrium, and there is an independent quantitative measure. When we deal wih social or political systems, we lack independent quantitative measures, although we quite often have qualitative measures. In either case, however, it is the law that explains the nonconforming as

12. See Kaplan, *Macropolitics,* pp. 234–36, 64–65.

well as the conforming event. The counterinstance is neither a denial of the law nor an exception to it, for the law holds only under the appropriate boundary conditions. This is true of all laws including those of physical science.

Normative and Predictive Theories

Long before the common language philosophers entered the game, Morris R. Cohen pointed out that scientific generalizations can be expressed either as predictive or as prescriptive. "Two atoms of hydrogen and one of oxygen combine under certain conditions to produce water" is an empirical predictive statement; but one can express it as a prescription: "If you want water, add hydrogen to oxygen under the stated conditions."

It is misleading, however, for Scriven to claim that counterexamples will not disprove statements in prescriptive form. In the case of given analytical or mathematical systems, if two plus two does not equal four or if adding two plus two does not produce four, we can state that the "twos" were wrongly identified or the wrong mathematical logic was applied. In the case of a scientific statement, if adding hydrogen to oxygen does not produce water, we can state that either a necessary boundary condition was not present or that some unknown boundary condition affected the experiment. However, if the boundary conditions are completely specified as is always the case in a good scientific theory, a counterexample will serve to disconfirm any given empirical hypothesis and its corollary prescription.

Some prescriptive statements deal entirely with conventional systems, as in games. For instance, the rules of poker specify that three kings beat three queens. In this case, a prescriptive statement is predictive only insofar as people play the game of "poker." If some individuals play according to different rules, we can only say either that they are not playing "poker" or that they are playing a variant of their own invention. Such prescriptions cannot be disproved; but that is so by definition. Some cases of rules are partly dependent upon purpose and partly empirical. For example, statements about corporations imply in part rules established by positive legal systems. On the other hand, the fact that groups of individuals acting in relation to selected physical entities behave organizationally is a statement confirmable by empirical observation. To the extent that empirical elements, whether universal or probabilistic, are involved in prescriptions concerning such mixed cases, they can be disproved.

Consider language. Some American Indian languages, for instance, have words that designate "rider-on-horse." These vocabularies fail to distinguish the rider as separable from the horse, at least in the accounts given by some anthropologists. If so, the statement that a language does not permit certain discriminations that can be made is an empirically testable proposition. (English, on the other hand, cannot express "man-on-horse" as a unit of behavior.)

In the case of the corporation, the empirically observed properties of behavior may in part be related to the legal definition of "corporation." That is, expectations flowing from the system of legal rights and obligations influence the behavior that is observed. The language example would find a better correlate in gangs or in other organizations that had no legal status, although even here nonlegal norms will affect behavior.

It is a characteristic of human prescriptive systems that they are related to human purposes. Thus, for instance, the purpose of scientific experiment is to explain observed events in a way that is independent of more particular desires. Legal analysis has a similar purpose. However, the way in which a legal system operates is not independent of particular purposes. Moreover, it can be changed. Whether legal systems are useful or good depends upon the kind of world one wants to live in. These considerations are more intimately related to human purpose than are other kinds of empirical scientific statements and can be treated scientifically in the empirical sense only by the method described in *Macropolitics*. Otherwise one can test these systems only for their conformity with procedural or substantive definitional criteria—thus, for instance, a system of law cannot depend merely upon the whim of an individual who is designated "judge"—or for consistency or for the actual consequences produced by the chosen rules.

The rules of empirical science can be shown to be incomplete if they cannot account for, or cannot regulate, a possible experiment. The rules of language are deficient for a given purpose if they cannot account for, or cannot regulate, a possible communicable observation to which reference is relevant. The rules of law, however, can be shown to be incomplete only if they do not permit a desired, and not merely a possible, legal discrimination. Indeed, a system of law that permits a possible but undesired discrimination is dysfunctional.

As the implementation of a system depends upon the conditions under which implementation occurs and as we can never know in advance the complete gamut of possibilities, our understanding of any particular enterprise such as mathematics or science or law or justice can never be known to be complete. As the interrelationships change—and they likely will change as conditions change—our understanding of the enterprise also changes to some degree. We cannot, for instance, say that science did not exist before relativity and quantum theory. Nonetheless our understanding of the methods, that is, of the rules, followed by science has changed as a consequence of these theories. Thus we can have a changed—and hopefully better—understanding both of the rules governing a discipline and of the substantive aspects of a discipline; and this is true of science or of mathematics as well as those disciplines such as law that include more particularistically purposive elements.

The common language philosophers believe that the fact that this rule-oriented process transcends any known preexisting set of rules implies a form of rational procedure that is neither analytical nor inductive. They merely mistake the process of discovery for that of confirmation. Every theory that can be expressed in a form susceptible to confirmation can be—indeed ideally must be—expressed within a deductive framework. Any set of legal norms can be expressed in terms of a deductive framework unless it is too complicated for this purpose. And, if the latter condition holds, this condition implies that the rules cannot be known to completely or consistently regulate behavior. Thus, any predictive or prescriptive theory, at the time of application, is, if possible, a closed system. On the other hand, with respect to identification, the substantive or procedural criteria something must meet to be, for instance, part of a system of law constitute a checklist. This list need not be deductive. We can reason about it in terms of closeness of "fit" and procedures of approximation. This latter reasoning process can involve deductive elements, often involving laws, although this is so usually in the "engineering" sense.

A major question is whether a theory sketch, that is, a loosely universalistic system of laws, accounts economically for the evidence—whether it fits. A particular theory may "fit" some real world situations but not others. This matter is not *merely* descriptive, however. For instance, with respect to my "balance of power" theory, the theory does not seem to describe the properties of events in Europe after 1870. The reasons for this are specified below. We would expect that in a "balance of power" system alliances would be short-lived, based on immediate interests, and neglectful of existing or previous alliance status. The rigid alliance systems of the European great nations between 1871 and 1914 and the relatively unlimited nature of World War I would seem, superficially at least, inconsistent with the prescriptions of the "balance of power" theory. We could, of course, resolve the problem by analyzing the period from 1871 to 1914 in terms of a rigid "balance of power" system. This solution, however, would require us to analyze every characteristically different state of the world in terms of a different systems model, thus depriving the concept of system of much of its theoretical meaning and turning it into a primarily descriptive device. The alternative procedure is to decide whether the underlying theory of the "balance of power" system can be used to explain the observed discrepancies.

We do not, of course, assert that if the theory of the "balance of power" system can account for the behavioral differences from 1871 to 1914, it therefore is *the* true explanation of the observations of system properties. Undoubtedly, other factors played important roles in producing both the specific properties of the sequence of events and the properties of the general form that the sequence took. We will merely have established that the asserted irregular properties do not invalidate—or are consistent with—the theory and that the theory may be useful for relating a wider range of observations than is possible in its absence. This may increase the confidence we place in the theory and its explanatory power.

The reconciliation of theory and observed properties follows. If we recognize, as there is reason to believe that Bismarck foresaw, that the seizure of Alsace-Lorraine by Prussia led to a public opinion in France that was ineluctably revanchist, this parameter change permits engineering the theory in a way consistent with the developments that followed. As long as Germany was unwilling to return Alsace-Lorraine to France, France would be Germany's enemy. Thus France and Germany became the poles of rigid, opposed alliances, as neither would enter—or at least remain in—the same coalition, regardless of other specific common interests. The chief motivation for limitation of war in the theoretical system is the need to maintain the existence of other essential actors as potential future allies. For the foreseeable future, however, neither France nor Germany was the potential ally of the other. Consequently, neither had an incentive—as would normally be the case in a "balance of power" system—to limit its war aims against the other. What had been an incentive for limitation became instead a disincentive. A somewhat analogous problem occurred with respect to the alignment pattern of the Italian city-state system. In this system, Florence, for a considerable period of time, functioned as the hub of opposed alignments. In the case of this system, the explanation involved a geographic factor.

These engineering examples need to be distinguished from the ordinary ad hoc use of hypotheses. As in the case of physics, which posits how bodies behave in a vacuum, my "balance of power" theory sketch examines how an international system will behave if states optimize external security. Both posits are often counterfactual. Nonetheless, it is possible to utilize such theories to explain what will happen under specific but different circumstances. In the case of the European "balance" after 1870, it can be established independently that French public opinion interfered in particular definite ways with the optimization of French external security. If these specific "starting states" of the system are engineered into the theory sketch, our predictions would be consistent with the actual behavior of the system. The difficulty is that we have not a complete theory but a theory sketch, that the boundary conditions and the confirming evidence are not completely stated, and that therefore the level of confidence in the explanation is low. The theory sketch, however, is consistent with what did occur and, everything else being equal, what happened is what one would have expected on the basis of the theory.

Moreover, these theory sketches can be falsified in principle. Thus, it can be shown that my "balance of power" theory correctly describes behavior during appropriate portions of the classic Greek city-state system. However, the explanation provided by the model is wrong. It can be shown by independent evidence that logistic (and some political) reasons played a far greater role than strategic reasons in the maintenance of system equilibrium. On the other hand, independent evidence can be adduced to show when the Italian city-states began to behave in accordance with the theory sketch for the reasons the theory would indicate. Thus, such theory sketches, although soft in the scientific sense, do come within the ambit of empirical science.

Categories of Explanation

We can now distinguish a number of different types of explanation in history: (1) A system of universal and sufficient relationships that rest on laws or at least on lawlike statements. They may be subsumed under general statements or they may be dispositional. These are theories in the strict sense and produce explanations in the strict sense. (2) A system of relationships that does not produce a univocal answer. The relationship between any particular prediction and the system of assumptions is plausible only. (3) The system of implications is not sufficiently precise to permit definite conclusions, although it excludes some. Both the reasoning process involved in this system of implications and the predictions asserted by the system are plausible only. The second and third categories constitute theory sketches rather than theories and permit only loose explanations. (4) We deal with identification, that is, with "what" explanations rather than "why" explanations: with fits (based on a variety of independent criteria) that are more or less close and that suggest analogies. This may occur intuitively or it may be conscious and rule regulated.

We have very few (probably no) instances in history that fall under category one. Those cases where prediction is genuinely possible depend either upon strong intuition or upon circumstances in which particular parameters dominate particular events. Why did Cortes conquer Baja California? Was it his ambition? Even with respect to "what" questions, how do we identify Cortes as an ambitious man? We must first have a theory about what constitutes ambition and how it will manifest itself under a large number of circumstances. Second, we must be able to distinguish types of ambition from each other, for the rubric undoubtedly covers many different kinds of personal characteristics that manifest themselves quite differently under different situations. Is it true, for instance, that the prediction that Cortes would have conquered Baja California is weaker than the retrodiction that he conquered it because of his ambition? His real reason may have had little or nothing to do with ambition; retrodiction is plausible at best. Is it so unlikely that someone living at the time of Cortes could have predicted that this particular man for one of a large number of reasons would have chosen just that particular route of conquest? Were the predictions, for instance, that Hitler would continue his territorial conquests of Europe, despite his public assertions to the contrary, on weaker ground than the explanations offered for his actions after the events?

Was my prediction at the beginning of the Cuban missile crisis that Khrushchev would back down weaker than the retrospective reasons offered for Khrushchev's decisions? These questions cannot be answered in general, for they depend upon the types of information that can be brought to bear on them, and these may differ from instance to instance with respect to whether the prediction or retrodiction is stronger. The question about whether the inference from the event to the cause or from the cause to the event is stronger depends upon how open the system of explanation is and how good the method of identification is.

Our attempts to deal with historical particularities almost always involve us in explanatory systems that are of the second, third, and fourth categories. As a consequence, the system of logical derivations and attributions or identifications permits us only to make plausible statements, although the closer the form within which the plausibility is expressed comes to the first category the greater the assurance we can have in our reasoning process.

Many of our interpretations of history rest on apparent plausibility. The structure of influence, however, often is of the third category and sometimes rests on a misuse of the principles of the fourth category. For instance, the Bible mentions instances of child sacrifice. Did these really occur? Some scholars believe they did not, because child sacrifice was not part of the culture and civilization of the ancient near East. But then child sacrifice is not part of the culture or civilization of contemporary India: yet it occurs in India. With respect to matters of this kind, one can usually believe what one wants to believe, for the evidence is sufficiently scanty so that competing conclusions are equally plausible. On matters of this kind we usually erect structures of explanation heavier than the weight of evidence they are designed to bear.

Sometimes, however, we merely ask the wrong questions. Thus, many assert that Lee Harvey Oswald was a bad shot and that he could not have fired off the bullets that killed President John F. Kennedy within the short time period required. They, however, are answering the question about whether they would have expected Lee Harvey Oswald to succeed in assassinating Kennedy under the given circumstances. They are not asking, as they should, whether in view of the success of the assassination, his solitary commission of the crime is more likely than any competing alternative. By asking the wrong question, they are incorrectly specifying the body of evidence that needs to be comprehended within the explanation. I am, for instance, an exceptionally poor billards player and yet on one occasion I had a run of three three-cushion billiard shots of the most difficult variety. A run of three in three-cushion billiards is very good even with respect to relatively easy shots. The improbability of an event is not evidence that it did not happen. A hand of thirteen spades in bridge is no more improbable than any other particular honestly dealt hand that any player has ever held. Any life history depends upon a combination of events so remote that the probability of its occurrence beforehand is virtually zero.

What must be shown about an event is that it is less probable than the competing alternatives, given the evidence available. Thus, in the case of Lee Harvey Oswald, given the knowledge that he had a weapon, that he was in the Texas book depository, and so forth, it is less improbable that on that particular day he got off two or three good shots than that other marksmen were participating in the event. However, much of historical interpretation rests upon the asking of incorrect questions concerning the probability of events, and it is too much to hope that this will change.

Explanations in history usually fall in the third category—the loosest sort of theory sketch—or the fourth category, which deals with facts and their interpretations. The logic of explanation is plausible at best, the derivations are not univocal, and the mapping operations that permit identification are both difficult to apply and subject to interpretation based on theories that themselves are of the third variety. One can grant that we do not use laws to explain these events, but our explanations are exceptionally poor.

Historical explanations are always overdetermined, at least when they deal with social and political events. The policy of a state may be related to constraints imposed by the nature of the international system, constraints imposed by technology and weapons systems, constraints imposed by the character of the domestic political system, constraints imposed by the bargaining coalitions that make up the government, constraints imposed by regime requirements, constraints imposed by personal relations, friendship, and personality, constraints imposed by purely accidental factors or the particular order within which information is received, and so forth. As a consequence, except in those cases where one particular constraint largely determines an outcome, the most we can say is that the event is consistent with what we would expect from the standpoint of a particular theoretical framework. Since we can never specify all the relevant frameworks and since we can never acquire all the information necessary to arrive at a conclusion, in particular information contained within the privacy of a decision-maker's mind, we can never know that we have a genuine explanation; we can only know that we have something that meets some of the criteria of an explanation and some degree of confidence that this is not an artifact.

Thus our interpretations may have to be revised drastically upon the discovery of new evidence. Or we may discover that our explanation of an event attributes design where accident played a major role, for example, Benes's casual suggestion to Stalin, on observing a demarcated map in his office, that the postwar Polish boundary with Germany be shifted from the Eastern to the Western Neisse.

A Summary

If one were to argue that every historical explanation can be put in the form of a precise deductive system, he would be wrong for a number of practical reasons. The system of relationships would be too complicated in many cases, and we would be unable to express the logic involved. The theoretical sketches from which parts of the explanations would be derived would be diverse and not assimilable within a single framework. Many of the procedures would involve "fitting" operations that cannot be employed as precisely as can the generalization for a two-body problem in iterated physical science calculations. Independent measures would not be available for some of the variables.

If, on the other hand, Scriven attempts to argue that the deductive form is inappropriate, he fails to understand that except for identification problems, and frequently even with respect to these (for they are often dependent upon theories concerning identification), our ability to formulate a statement capable of explaining an event depends upon our ability to articulate it within a reasoned system. To the extent that we are incapable of doing this, our answers are not good answers, even though they may be the best that we can achieve. Even though we do not have real theories or laws in social science—at least yet—we do have some theory sketches and explanations of a looser sort.

Many of the circumstances in which we live provide a sufficiently common environment such that we take the boundary conditions for granted and state occurrences within them as if they were not time bound, or at least not bound to the conditions providing the parameters. In such cases, we get good results if we predict as if changes at the boundary would not occur. In these cases, we have partial explanations that work. We can state why, for instance, political and social organization has been achieving greater complexity over time. We can state certain things in respect to biological evolution over time. We can state why certain things happen as they do within underdeveloped systems and why certain kinds of transformations are likely to occur in those systems over time. These may not be fully predictable, that is, univocally predictable, for reasons we have already stated; but we do have a kind of knowledge. A change at the boundary of a system—which might involve very large increases in population, or certain changes in food intake or in pollution—might entirely undermine these reasonable expectations. Or it might merely reshape these expectations within the framework of a broadened explanatory framework that includes both cases. Relativity theory, for instance, does this with Newtonian mechanics. In this respect, therefore, the social sciences are not so different from the physical sciences, for we can never know for sure what the laws of physics are dependent upon. There may always be some other process of which we are unaware that is slowly transforming the structure of the laws. We can never know the generalizations we employ to be universal; we merely treat them as if they are universal. The differences between the social and physical sciences are a matter of degree—even though the degree in this case is extremely important. The expectation that some boundary variable that we are unfamiliar with may be producing instability in what seems like a stable system of behavior is much higher in the social sciences than in the physical sciences. The important differences, however, involve those we have previously discussed: complicated interrelationships among the variables, a lack of independently measured equalities, and an absence of theories in the strict sense. Yet these differences are not differences of principle. They are matters of practice. Moreover, things we now regard as purely physical, for instance, complicated robots, and their societies, would also be subject to the same restrictions; thus the limitation is not a product of biological variables. And some areas of physical science manifest a similar resistance to theory and to explanation in the strict sense.

A SUMMARY

2

Historical Consciousness and Truth

Hegel, Marx, and Human Consciousness

When Marx said that he stood Hegel on his head, he did not mean to imply that Hegel was a subjective idealist. According to Hegel, the ideas of men devlop in their social milieu. Human consciousness is historical consciousness that involves the reaction of human beings to their surroundings. If the *Geist* works through men, it does not whisper directly into their ears. Consciousness, however, is not a mere reflection of one's surroundings. It does not develop apart from, or without being conditioned by, self-conscious knowledge of the present in relation to the past and to spirit or essence. Moreover, although the *Geist* works itself out in history, history is the realm of accident according to Hegel.[1] Accidents might ironically produce

1. In my view an accident is something not accounted for by the theoretical perspective that is in use. See Kaplan, *Macropolitics,* pp. 10, 11.

73

what the *Geist* requires, and men might produce something other than what they have consciously pursued.

As Hegel's idealism was an objective idealism, the world was not spun out of man's consciousness in his philosophy. Rather, man's consciousness was produced in the world. Hegel's philosophy was characterized as idealistic because the world was explainable according to intelligible concepts. History developed according to intelligible ideas that fell into a pattern. It was the Absolute that worked itself out in history despite accident, that became phenomenologically limited and subject to error during the processes of history, and that overcame error through time.

When Marx said that he stood Hegel on his head, he meant only that the social conditions of human life were regarded by him as the ultimate ground of reality rather than, as in Hegel's philosophy, merely an intermediary ground that represented a deeper underlying process. It would have perhaps been more accurate for Marx to have said that he removed the core of Hegel's philosophy and then restated it. Even this may be an overstatement, for Marx retained the dialectic and the concept of contradiction—elements involving logic (although not formal logic). Marx described himself as a materialist whose methods were used to discover whatever order existed in the material world rather than an immanent and global idealistic order; however, Hegel, as noted, was an objective idealist. When he said the real was the rational, he was talking about neither the existential world nor the human mind. According to Hegel, human ideas arose in relation to the existential world.

Marx argued against the simple inclusive pattern of Hegel's philosophy of history. Yet his own use of the dialectic seemed to impose upon the world a pattern of development which, although more complex perhaps than Hegel's and based upon more extensive historical research, in the end seems to impose on history a monocausal progression that seems like the unfolding of an idealistic scheme. Marx's concept of true self-knowledge also seems redolent of essence.

Clearly the interpretation of Marx offered above is highly controversial. Yet, there remained elements of similarity in the two philosophies that are related to Marx's concept of ideology. In Hegel's dialectical logic, reality contains contradictory (not merely inconsistent) elements. Although each phase of history overcomes the errors of the past, each new phase introduces errors of its own, which themselves are overcome in succeeding phases of history. Thus historical consciousness is always limited and always ideological; it can be overcome only by the overcoming of history. According to Marx, this occurs with the classless society because classes are the motor of history. By definition, those who understand how this final phase of history will work itself out, and who thus overcome history, possess not a false consciousness, or an ideology, but instead true scientific knowledge. Here, however, Marx breaks with Hegel, for he introduces an apocalyptic view of history in which there is a grand climax that is reached when the proletariat attains self-consciousness and revolutionizes society, rather than a constant and unending development of the march of God through history. Marx's view is thus more radical than Hegel's, especially in its epistemology.

Marx, unlike Lenin, had an activist theory of truth. We learn about things by acting upon them. This is made particularly clear in his theses on Feuerbach. Yet the attributes of reality can be experienced directly and described accurately, although only by one who is writing from the correct historical and sociological perspective. Reality is plastic in the sense that man is not bound by arbitrarily imposed laws, such as those of capitalism, which represent an imposition by a dominant class.

Nonideological Perception

Nonideological perception was not possible earlier in history—or to someone writing from the wrong class position—because the social reality that was represented in consciousness was itself in error or distorted. Once the correct perspective is found, however, false history ceases, for its motor power—class struggle based on false consciousness—is dissolved. Once truth is obtained, there are no errors to be overcome. Man will have left the realm of necessity and will have entered the kingdom of freedom—a kingdom unlimited by human need, by human error, or by external scarcity.

Marx and Hegel, however, held in common the explanation of the process by means of which past historical errors were inevitably overcome in history. This view was not genuinely paradoxical, although it did give rise to a debate in the early twentieth century. "Why if history is inevitable do people have to help it along?" was the question often asked in Russia. The correct response to this question within the Hegelian framework is that knowledge of external reality, including knowledge of error and moral failures, changes men's consciousness in such ways that they desire to overcome the past and to build the future. Thus, in both Hegelian and the Marxian systems there was no argument that events were inevitable apart from human action; rather, certain kinds of changes were inevitable in part at least because human beings would respond to the injustices of the present by developing the motivations that would lead them to act for change. A considerable part of Marxian theory was devoted to explaining how the motivations of different classes would change as capitalism developed. According to Marx, the search for profit in a capitalistic system, because of declining profits, would lead to the concentration and the socialization of industry, after which people would be motivated to work for and capable of achieving socialism. Although Marx hardly thought this process reversible, he never denied the intervention of motivation as a factor in its successful completion.

In Marx's view, great men cannot make history, because the lines of possible historical change are set by the (unconsciously) imposed economic limitations established by class interests. Thus a great man can only determine when the change occurs rather than what the change is. Yet it is difficult to explain the Russian Revolution if Marx was correct, for Russia did not move toward communism through developed capitalism. Was not Lenin a great man in this sense? Marx can also be challenged by showing his basic theory of economic determinism to be wrong in one of its major features. If a larger number of modal forms of economy are possible than Marx understood, if the relationships between the economy and political control systems are more complicated than Marx thought, or if his theory of value is wrong, then one has knocked away the framework within which he argues against the importance of great men in history with respect to anything except the timing of change.

The problem that Engels struggles with toward the end of his life, involving the relationship of the superstructure of ideas to the materialistic underpinning of history, is merely an illustration of the larger problem in which Marx's simplistic view of reality enmeshed itself. Marx imposed on history a monocausal framework: a framework of economic development. The problem is not whether changes in this framework require self-conscious activity, for in both the Marxian and Hegelian systems they do, but whether all of social reality can be encompassed within such a restrictive framework.

I have argued repeatedly against that point of view. Even if Marx's theory (at best theory sketch) of economic development is a good theory—and it is not—it would be unlikely that the variables included within it would be sufficiently dominant at all times and in all places to derive the remainder of social relations from them.

Even if we desire to use such a word as *material,* it does not follow that all material relations are economic. The world of material reality includes people and nature and buildings and even institutions. As both Charles Sanders Peirce and Morris R. Cohen never tired of pointing out, both things and relations exist in reality, although not necessarily in the same way. Relations are not merely categories of mind. The social system, the family system, the religious system, the political system, along with art and music and literature and so forth, are also part of social and historical reality. Marx's materialistic set of categories rests upon a drastic decision. He simply eliminated everything that did not fit within his framework of explanation.

There are many interpretations of Marx, besides Engels's version, and perhaps versions by Marx himself (not merely the young and the old). We have no desire to choose one interpretation as authentic. Marx dealt often with the problem of reification under conditions of capitalism. If self-conscious man could eliminate all reifications, as Marx sometimes seemed to suggest, and if he could treat his environment and his society as infinitely plastic, he would have achieved the kind of "absolute freedom" Hegel rejected as meaningless death. Whether Marx really intended to reach this conclusion or not, he wrote at times as if he had a total theory, not dependent on parameters, from which all can be deduced. According to this view, man can make his own true history, free of reifications and of constraints. This, of course, is a romantic illusion (which we will discuss briefly in the next chapter). Although structure (form) may be viewed as more slowly changing process—the physiological system also changes over time—the ability to think and to act depends upon the existence of a framework within which acts are meaningful and productive. No framework can be changed except through the employment of some other framework. There is no society without roles and role relationships, and even the Russians seem to be learning that marginal analysis is not peculiar to capitalism.

If the previous interpretation of Marx is correct, he grievously overestimated the plasticity of society and of the economy. He misunderstood that in the absence of form, only indescribable chaos ensues. Even change is a change from one form to another and thereby implies constraint. Self-consciouness cannot rise above form, for thought requires form and rule if it is to be expressed.

If Marx is interpreted (more favorably) as arguing only that some forms can be replaced by others, then his theory pretends to offer a total and fully deductive explanation. Freedom (and we will return to this subject in the next chapter) then lies in a greater harmonization between the forms of society and the potential autonomy of man. Precisely, however, because Marx's framework of analysis is so restricted, his conclusions reflect his monocausal premises.

The Nature of Ideology
Ideology and philosophy have at least one function in common. They attempt to give coherence to the universe in which we live. We do not approach the world with blank minds. We have codes for identi-

fication and implicit hypotheses with which we approach the world. We attempt to give meaning to our life by encompassing such elements within a coherent explanatory framework.

Do propitiatory practices bring rain? Does acting nicely toward another person bring rewards? Will listening to absurd demands appease anger? Will censorship depress the level of immoral behavior? We approach life with limited information and a great need to arrive at decisions. We operate on analogy and on metaphor in the absence of better methods.

The search for analogies appropriate to decision-making leads to the imposition of a degree of coherence on reality that is at least not known to be genuinely present but that, at best, in the present state of knowledge, provides us with first-order approximations that enable us to act.

If we wish to label the process of approaching reality through approximations ideological, we can. But, if so, then all views of all people are ideological. Most individuals, however, learn to differentiate, to use first-order approximations as only first-order approximations and to revise their beliefs with respect to individual areas of activity as information increases. Most belief systems are therefore permeable. As knowledge increases, belief systems become differentiated. They cease to be interpreted in terms of one putatively coherent theoretical sketch. On the other hand the richness of the interconnections between the different sketches increases while inconsistencies and ad hoc or "forced" consistencies diminish.

Some individuals, however, have less permeable belief systems than others; they develop methods for screening out information that does not conform with their first approximations; they overlook inconsistencies in their reasoning process; they account for discrepancies between believed predictions and observed events by increasingly complicated series of ad hoc explanations or by ignoring the difficulties. The pattern of explanation is increasingly "force-fitted." These are what I would prefer to call ideological belief systems.

Ideological belief systems often have powerful psychological appeal, for they offer answers to questions that people feel a need to ask. They give the impression of power with respect to the world, for they are believed to represent a key to the unlocking of nature. They are the philosopher's stone of the social sciences. They aspire to solve all problems, often by implicit definition and by over-generalization. Thus, it can be believed that capitalism exploits, and that, because of the declining rate of interest, a capitalist nation will seek colonies and engage in war. Although Israel really has many socialistic features, by these restricted definitions it is capitalistic. It is therefore imperialistic and therefore exploits the Arabs who by definition are colonized.

The Marxian system in most current practices is ideological, as I use that term, not simply because it contains inaccurate hypotheses or useless definitions, but because it holds on to these rigidly and thus short-circuits a process of investigation that permits greater articulation and the rectification of previously held beliefs.

Perspectives and Scientific Knowledge

Knowing always involves a relationship between a perceiver and a perceived. The human organism as an instrument of perception codes incoming information. If negative feedback operates, that is, if the code or parts of it can be corrected, the organism can overcome selectively distortions of perception. Although the process is never independent of the instrumentation employed, it does permit public and objective knowledge. For example, to a perceiving instrument with a span of perception of a fraction of a second the stars are constant and the planets moving. To a creature with a span of perception of thousands of years the planets would be a circle of light and the stars would be perceived as moving. Yet, it is important to recognize that both perceptions refer to truths about the external world and that they are expressible within the framework of a single language.

Our astronauts can fly through the path of a heavenly body without colliding with it. This confirms the truth of our particular perception. If, however, one were able to pass through the path of a planetary body with a vehicle traveling at a slow enough speed, collision would occur, thereby confirming the second perception. Both of these apparently contradictory statements are expressible in a form that resolves the "contradiction."

The Vietnamese villager on whose house a bomb falls may see the war in Vietnam as one producing destruction of civilians. The Vietcong soldier may see it as a struggle against imperialism. The supporter of the government in Saigon may see it as an effort to prevent Communist tyranny. The executive in Washington may see it as part of an effort to impede the progress of totalitarianism and to protect American strategic interests. It is possible for all these perceptions to be correct simultaneously, depending upon the definitions of the key terms and appropriate qualifications. It is, moreover, possible for someone to write an account of the war that comprehends these different frameworks and places them in perspective.

How do we perform the mapping operations that permit us to comprehend divergent or at least different points of view within a common explanatory framework? Does a teacher, for instance, see things differently from a student? But how do we know that there are teachers and students? Perhaps Mr. Jones sees himself as a teacher and Johnny Smith sees him as a jailor. Is a laborer a member of the proletariat? Perhaps a laborer sees himself as a potential capitalist. It is surely an advance in interpretation of the situation if we can get second-order agreement.

Perhaps the student can see that the teacher sees himself as a teacher within a socially defined role with definite societal purposes. Perhaps the teacher, on the other hand, can see the student as a person who has no desire to learn to read and write and to acquire a job but as a person who desires to go out into the field and to gambol. At least with respect to this student, he may be functioning as a jailor, despite his own intention and despite the socially defined role he occupies. On the other hand, the teacher may have had experience with many students like this particular one who felt they did not want to acquire education and who later regretted their lack of it. Can he show to the particular student that he is misperceiving his own desires when these are considered over a longer time span? And if the teacher cannot make the demonstration to the student, could he make it to an impartial observer, at least with respect to statistical probability?

When Britain and France were negotiating with the Soviet Union in the summer of 1939, should it really have been so difficult for them to perceive the advantages to the Soviet Union of a deal with Nazi Germany? Could they not have achieved second-order agreement on a listing of Soviet objectives and available alternatives?

Consider the case of a class of students shown pictures of people. Their teachers are told in some cases that the people are intelligent and in other cases that they are stupid or in some cases that they are rich and in other cases that they are poor. The teachers do not overtly communicate this information to the pupils, but the pupils' judgments turn out to be largely consistent with what the teachers were told. Perception is distorted by expectation. Yet, we can make these statements only because we know that the students' perceptions do distort something. Moreover, if we can discover the subliminal methods by means of which the misinformation is imparted, we can even demonstrate the process by means of which the distortion occurs.

When Marx or Mannheim talk about class bias, or class viewpoint, are they saying more than that individuals tend not to perceive things similarly from different perspectives? Chamberlain and Daladier did not correctly perceive Stalin's objectives, but other people did. We can state what we mean when we say their perceptions distorted Stalin's options. We can thus obtain second-order agreement.

If someone says labor is being exploited and if more laborers than capitalists believe this, is that the end of scientific inquiry? Can we define what we mean by exploitation? If by exploitation we mean unequal division of societal production, then labor is being exploited. If, on the other hand, we mean by exploitation that labor receives less than its input into the productive process, there are standards in economic theory for the determination of this, even though they are somewhat less than precise or easily agreed upon. Even so, at the worst, they exclude certain inferences and narrow the range of reasoned difference. If the worker says, yes, I am not being exploited within a marginal analysis framework, but I do not like the framework, again we have second-order agreement.

The second-order agreements are always limited, for they involve judgments on the relationships of variables within the real world and agreed definitions for the uses of words. As we have already discussed, a knowledge of the former depends upon boundary conditions not all of which are known to us. Historical consciousness has its limits, but it also possesses self-transcending properties.

Marx employed a closed model. He assumed that history was determined by a particular factor. Thus he distinguished between true consciousness, which involved a correct perspective with respect to the end of the process, and false consciousness which reflected the interests of particular sociological placement. Most historicists reduced everything to perspective, but they eliminated the possibility of true consciousness.

What can a perspective be if we cannot state the standpoint from which the perspective exists, what it depends upon, and what it leaves out of account? Yet, to the extent we can do this, we can comprehend different perspectives and, to that extent, transcend them.

The reality about which we are trying to achieve second-order agreement is complex. There is no single perspective that exhausts it. And there is no single perspective from which any particular individual is tied to it. A man functions in the economy, in the political system, in a family, in leisure activities, and so on. He functions as a citizen of the state and also as a citizen in the world. In modern society, at least, he is attuned to different perspectives. Even members of construction unions can be made aware that the featherbedding activities in which they engage raise greatly the cost of housing for the rest of us. We may differ about whether this is wise or unwise, just or unjust. But surely we can get second-order agreement on the fact that costs are imposed upon the rest of us.

We can distinguish between a situation in which an individual's interests are tied so closely to a particular one of the systems in which he is involved that he cannot easily separate them and a situation in which they are not tied so closely. We can distinguish between the existence of a situation in which they are tightly bound and the desirability or undesirability of that situation.

An individual may be capable of seeing that his interests as they develop over time are tied to the maintenance of a particular status quo. At the same time, he may be able to recognize, not only that others might prefer a situation in which that status quo is not maintained, but that if he had it to do all over again with free opportunity and choice, he himself might prefer a different status quo. As such distinctions are made, the range of second-order agreement increases and extends to the categorization and perhaps even to the listing of preferences.

The "Is" and the "Ought"

With respect to arriving at second-order (or possibly even first-order) agreements, there are two frameworks to be considered: that of the "is" and that of the "ought." The "is" for all practical purposes is independently determinable in many respects despite the skewed perceptions of most people. Thus, for instance, Marx's prediction of the impoverishment of the working classes has clearly been disproved. Except for ideologies, that is, closed systems of thought, minimal feedback serves to answer many questions of this kind. Many perspectives or perceptions that people have of the "is" do not deal with matters that are so unambiguous; therefore it is possible for them to persist more easily because of environmentally determined misperceptions. However, the expansion of the framework of knowledge, especially when pursued self-consciously, permits greater and greater correction. It permits us to determine better the parameters that determine system behavior. With respect to questions concerning the "ought," the expansion of the framework of perspective over time permits greater understanding of the factors that lead people to develop the moral preferences they have. Expansion of such perspectives enables us to learn the factors upon which such preferences are dependent. This permits us to acquire a common framework within which discussion of preferences and of their foundations is at least possible.

We can develop certain intersubjectively appealing principles of justice and fair play, for instance, the principle of generalization or of universalization that in turn enable us to get increasingly better perspectives on moral questions, even in many cases where substantive agreement is not present. Since, however, moral or "ought" questions involve the internal states of the perceiving systems in a more radical fashion than do questions concerning the "is," most writers do not regard these matters as capable of objective scientific determination. I have argued in *Macropolitics* that questions concerning the truth of moral propositions are empirically meaningful, and I have provided suggestions concerning thought experiments that might deal with them. Even though I have no great confidence that such experiments can be carried out, the difficulties appear to lie largely in the realm of practice.[2] Thus even with respect to the "ought," I would argue that there are empirical and objective foundations for beliefs concerning the validity of morals. Although I can only adumbrate the position here, it deals essentially with man as a multistable system that is structured to optimize certain values. The system operates under conditions of imperfect information and limited means. As a consequence, it uses pathological responses that provide secondary gains, but nonetheless it tries to improve both its own outcomes and the environmental framework through which they are pursued. Man therefore has a tendency to pursue justice. His verbal prescriptive claims are related to this aspect of his structure. Although this complicated position has been only briefly sketched here, it is meaningful in the ordinary sense of empirical science.

I do not deny that individuals' needs are related to

2. See Morton A. Kaplan, *Macropolitics,* pp. 36ff., 135ff.

their life situations. Most individuals find it difficult to think beyond these circumstances and rationalize their needs as universal prescriptions. Some individuals, however, can understand that they would see things differently from other social perspectives in a given society and still differently if they could construct a different social order. It is this possibility and the process to which it gives rise that provides in part at least a possibility of social melioration. This in part provides a tension toward justice. Again, however, this topic is treated at greater length in *Macropolitics*.

The Growth of Perspective

As we pursue a subject scientifically, we construct for ourselves a wider and wider comparative web for the interpretation of aspects of history. Of course, mere quantitative increase is not sufficient; modes of questioning that plumb qualitatively different aspects of the subject matter, that systematically probe different perspectives and different points of view, provide us, not with a single coherent explanation or a single interpretation of history, but with a much wider comparative framework within which to formulate a perspective from any particular point of view.

Perhaps the phrase "the truth of history" is itself too strong; perhaps history provides us instead with "truths." Yet even these "truths" illuminate matters for us successfully only to the extent that our knowledge of the context from which the "truth" is seen enables us to evaluate it against other perspectives and other "truths." We increase knowledge through different and better approximations. We see more deeply, for instance, whether conflicts were as irreconcilable as the participants saw them or whether more adequate information or more benign circumstances might have permitted compromise or even concordance. We understand better whether the individuals were caught within the web of a system structure that constrained their freedom to find their way out or whether they created the danger that engulfed them through misunderstanding or intemperance. If excessive understanding of the situations and motivations of others may at times prevent the statesman from acting promptly and energetically to solve a problem, the failure to inform himself by comparing different systems or periods prevents the student of history from understanding adequately the motives that led men and the situations that confronted them.

Santayana said that the failure to understand history condemns men to repeating it; the failure to study history comparatively prevents men from understanding it. No period can ever make sense only in its own terms, for although the perspective provided from within a situation does provide some illumination, it ignores the context that made the situation what it was and that differentiated it from all the alternatives that might otherwise have existed.

Although we can never know what a particular situation truly is dependent upon, for we can never exhaust the range of alternatives, we can obtain from history deeper and wider perspectives concerning this; the social sciences at least should provide us with cumulative knowledge. Properly employed—truistic explanation is not the proper employment—comparative study will enlighten us. We can know ourselves at least as much, or perhaps more, from what we are not as from what we are.

The theoretical perspectives from which history can be viewed have power to illuminate the actions of men as they vary with place and conditions. Even if a theory is internally consistent and a good theory for the particular system to which it is applied, it may explain only part of the variance of the problem. Sometimes a particular perspective plays only a minor role in an explanatory pattern. For instance, some claim that the United States is in Vietnam for economic profit. Although the stockmarket reactions when peace seems nearer contraindicate this assertion for the economy at large, it may explain the motivations of some individuals or of some businesses. British interest in the Middle East for a long time, for instance, was strongly responsive to oil. On the other hand, strategic considerations, other political motives, and other values played a role in their decision processes. It is possible for the motivation resulting from a particular theoretical perspective to move a person or a nation toward particular types of decisions and yet for those decisions to be made otherwise for countervailing reasons. For instance, the British more recently have been withdrawing from the Persian Gulf area. Examples are always treacherous because people can always disagree about them; the greater danger, however, lies in assuming that any particular theoretical perspective produces almost all the variance to be explained in an individual's or a nation's behavior.

In the political and social sciences we cannot isolate those aspects of the variables with which we desire to deal. The physicist would be hard put to intuit his universal laws if the physical entities he had to work with were contaminated by the operation of large numbers of variables belonging to other disciplines. Even in the physical laboratory, the scientist has to assume that a research assistant has not engaged in mischief; and there has been embarrassment for some important scientists as a result of such mischief. We assume that the controlled physical conditions really do exist and overlook the factors their existence may be dependent upon. At least, however, the physicist can usually attempt to specify boundary conditions completely. (Many things in the world are not relevant to any experiment.) In the social sciences, we cannot even attempt to do this in the absence of comparative method. It is only through the systematic application of comparative method that we are able even to explore boundary problems and their consequences for system behavior in at least a semireasonable manner.

It is thus through comparative method that we are able to rise above Mannheim's relativism, and it is through comparative method, rather than the vantage point of a single correct perspective, as in Marx, that we approach correct understanding. Insofar as we employ theory sketches rather than theories, insofar as our knowledge of boundary conditions and our specifications of relevant evidence are known to be incomplete, the level of confidence in our explanations will be low. Yet it is only through the self-conscious use of comparative theory sketches that we can articulate our reasoning sufficiently, specify boundary conditions reasonably, and begin to specify relevant evidence. Thus, to the extent that scientific theory can be applied to history and to politics, comparative methods are required.

Irony and Meaning
Much of what bemuses the historian in terms of irony or tragedy may simply result from a failure of appropriate system reference. Hegel refers to the cun-

ning of history. Consider the case of the wheat farmer who sees the price of wheat going down and raises more wheat. This is surely a sensible decision from the standpoint of the individual wheat farmer. Yet as each wheat farmer makes the same decision independently, production of wheat increases and the price decreases, thus for practical purposes leaving each farmer where he started, although each has worked harder. This is ironic perhaps, but one does not need a historical *Geist* to explain it. That individuals often produce the opposite of what they intend, that results are often inadvertent, or that accidents often determine history is not something that should surprise anyone.

The Yugoslav coup of 1940 and Mussolini's attack upon Greece were among the events that prevented Hitler's conquest of the Soviet Union. They were not inevitable, and it was not inevitable that free nations would win out. But, on the other hand, there is no underlying irony of history that necessarily produced these results.

Much of history is absurd; it is misleading to attempt to account for much of history according to any single intellectual idea. History is a realm within which many different theoretical frameworks combine to overdetermine events. History is not the working out of freedom on earth. It is not even the increase of complexity on earth. In this sense, history has no meaning except the meaning it has for individuals within the contexts of the matters that have importance for them. The defeat of Hitler meant that some Jews could survive on the continent of Europe. The defeat of Hitler meant that reasonably democratic regimes could be restored in Great Britain and France. The defeat of Hitler meant that the Soviet Union would dominate much of Eastern Europe. The meaning of the dropping of an atomic weapon on Hiroshima was that a quarter of a million Japanese were incinerated. It also meant that Japan would surrender and be re-born as a democracy. But all we mean when we say that history had these meanings is that these were consequences of particular chains of events within particular contexts of interpretation.

The search for meaning in history, except in the limited sense in which it has just been described, is in fact part of an effort to impose upon history a single schema that it cannot possibly bear. It is equivalent to the search for the ether in physics, for there is no more an absolute history in which historical events occur than there is an ether in which physical events occur. History has no independent existence. Nor is there any unity that can single-mindedly be imposed upon it, for history is analyzable from many different perspectives that can be applied only within limited frameworks.

IRONY AND MEANING

The search for laws of history is a cul de sac, for it implies a system of sufficient coherence for it to have a biography. If there were laws of history, the following things would have to be true. We would have to be able to build the large array of variables from culture, politics, technology, economics, and so forth, into a single theory (or at least theoretical sketch). Yet there is no general theory of economics and certainly not of politics. Except at the useless truistic level, our theories of politics apply only to specifiable types of political systems. Even worse, it would have to be true that all historical variables would have to be related to either a definite progression or to a definite cycling process, or to both; otherwise, the part systems would have relative independence, and laws, if any, would apply only within the specific sciences. In short, if there were laws of history, much of the previous parts of this book would be wrong.

If we deny that there are laws about history, how do we account for the apparent cycles in history that have been suggested by different students of the subject? For instance, Sorokin finds a cycle of sensate, ideational, and idealistic cultures. Although there is perhaps some reason to quarrel with the coding devices that Sorokin used, in general there do appear to have been recurring cycles of this kind. In past ages they apparently did not affect the great mass of people, but they apparently did occur at elite levels.

It may merely be that there are a limited number of forms within which intellectual and artistic efforts can be expressed. It then may be that the great innovations in those forms can occur only in the early stages of the cycle. In this case the later stages of the cycle become elaborations on themes. If this is the case, one might expect the elaborations eventually to play themselves out and to drive people seeking originality into new directions. It is also possible that there are certain reasons of economy that we do not fully understand that impart a regularity to the phases of the cycle.

When one deals with some political manifestations of such cycles, for instance, the phases of romanticism and of rationality in political styles, it is possible that as any style begins to be applied to the political world, it overcomes the difficulties of the past, shows great promise, and generates enthusiasm. Then it begins to create new problems—or at least old problems become increasingly manifest—and the advantages that it provides are taken for granted and the evils it overcame forgotten.

If this is so, and this is merely a speculation, then generative cycles of this kind, although hardly inevitable, might be quite likely. Although one cannot ignore the claim that the most recent romantic cycle is the consequence of television—and certainly the impact of television on the political process or on views of the world ought not to be overlooked—this explanation is perhaps a bit of an oversimplification. The romantic cycle in the early nineteenth century went very deep, as did that of the 1920s and 1930s as expressed in Italian fascism, German Nazism, the Spanish Falange, and the Japanese Black Dragon Society.

Attacks upon bourgeois corruption, upon calculation, and upon so-called linear reasoning pervaded all these movements before the origins of television, and, in the case of the early nineteenth-century romantic movements in Germany, even before the movies.

Others have noticed certain phase or cycle relationships in political phenomena, for instance, in purge processes. These might have been observed in the French Revolution, in Russia during the twenties and thirties, in China after the Communist revolution, and even in Burma in the areas controlled by the Communist rebels. The purges start slowly. There is an increase in numbers of people purged and in the degree of terror until a high point is reached. Then the process declines and finally ends. In this case, it is probable that we merely lack sufficiently good systems analyses. There is probably something in the internal dynamics of the purge in terms of the political pressures that it sets off, in terms of the needs of the leadership and of the pressures put upon potential oppositionists that intensifies the cycle. Then there is probably something in the way in which the process interferes with orderly administration and production that creates counterneeds. At the same time the terror of the purge has probably produced the required effects with respect to political passivity on the part of counterelites and the public.

This is speculation, and it should not be taken too seriously in the absence of detailed analysis, but it indicates, as in the case of the cultural cycles, that these are not genuinely independent historical processes, but separable aspects of historical continuity that can be studied with the techniques of the social sciences. If so, in principle, there are laws relating observable properties under specifiable boundary conditions.

Historical Ambiguity

It is precisely because the process of the identification of variables and the application of theories in history is so inherently ambiguous that we are likely to get extremely large numbers of the kinds of pathological observations that Langmuir found in some cases in the physical sciences. It is relatively easy to observe what one wants to or expects to observe. And precisely because our social alter egos interact self-consciously with us, we can create frameworks of shared expectations. We can to some extent create our own individual and national characters as we go along, by misinterpreting events, by responding in ways of our own invention.

Unfortunately the "mirror image" metaphor is not sufficiently explanatory, for sometimes, and perhaps often, the social structure is one in which our expectations ironically set the social system going in a different direction, as in the case of the wheat farmer who grows more wheat to make more money but who instead drives the price down or in the case of the "mark" whose trusting behavior brings out the cupidity in the card shark. To the extent, however, that we can create a climate of shared expectations and behavior, we do create situations in which the theorem of restricted choice gains applicability. Insofar as this occurs, the shared framework permits a kind of social stability that would not be possible in its absence. Yet irony plays its role here also. In system-dominant systems,[3] behavior that violates the rules or shared expectations may or may not produce particular gains but is extremely unlikely to change the system; in subsystem-dominant systems, a single important actor may change the type of the system by breaking the framework of expectations. In this latter case the shared expectations that normally make

3. See Kaplan, *Macropolitics,* pp. 66–67, for a definition of system and subsystem dominance.

for stability may in turn become a snare that permits a deviant actor to upset the system.

The uses that are made of history will be no better than the questions put to it. Knowledge of the applicability of different perspectives will enable one to ask better questions. But one's values or desires may nonetheless interfere with asking the right questions. Thus, during the discussions in 1949 preceding the decisions on whether to build an H-bomb, the General Advisory Committee of the Atomic Energy Commission advised against it, in part on the ground that fusion weapons would make inefficient use of nuclear resources. Later, when the so-called Teller invention changed these prospects, the GAC changed its position. Yet, it had asked the wrong questions in its original decision. It was irrelevant to show that the then known techniques for making fusion weapons from fissionable materials made inefficient use of these materials. The question was not whether one should build a stockpile of fusion bombs but whether one should use some fissionable materials for experimental purposes. A technological breakthrough such as occurred was not unlikely. As it was, the Soviet Union had a usable fusion weapon before the United States had; any further delay on the part of the United States might have been disastrous. The scientists had obviously asked the wrong questions; it is speculative why they did so. Perhaps they had guilt feelings over the Hiroshima and Nagasaki explosions or perhaps certain fears concerning the arms race. Their values almost assuredly influenced the conclusions they reached. Nonetheless nothing in their values forced them to ask the wrong questions, although the ambiguity of history encourages such error. On the other hand, the errors they entered into were avoidable and objectively analyzable.

There is a tendency, perhaps ineluctable given the needs of human beings for orientation in the world, to impose upon events excessively restrictive hypotheses and exceedingly unsatisfactory theory sketches. Thus with respect to the Soviet bloc, for instance, theory sketches of permanent purges alternate with those of societal changes toward freedom or even, in some cases, toward democracy. The intellectual difficulty of such theory sketches does not lie in the incorrectness of either. Either may turn out to be fortuitously correct. The difficulty lies in the almost casual assignment to reality of a prediction that pertains only to a model, whether implicit or explicit, that neglects many of the variables that will affect the real world outcome and that is blind to the sports that produce novelty—in other words, the difficulty lies in the use of the kinds of truisms that Scriven recommends.

It is amazing how often overly simple models are offered as conventional wisdom even in the face of contrary evidence. Thus, for instance, the Kennan-Fulbright thesis proposes that the way to produce favorable change in the Soviet bloc is to be friendly to individual bloc countries and to aid them. Yet, Yugoslavia broke with the Soviet bloc in 1948 during the period when American hostility toward Yugoslavia was even greater than toward the Soviet Union; China broke with the Soviet Union during the period in which American hostility toward China was greater than toward the Soviet Union; Rumania developed autonomy during a period in which American citizens were not even permitted to travel to Rumania; Poland has been the most retrogressive of all the Communist bloc nations since 1956, and it has been the recipient of large amounts of American aid and friendship.

The Kennan-Fulbright thesis is usually buttressed by the seemingly commonsensical — or in Scriven's vocabulary, truistic—argument that the advocated policy provides Communist governments with alternatives. But with what kinds of alternatives does it provide them? Did American aid perhaps reduce Polish need for increased economic productivity, for the consensus underlying such productivity, and therefore for less repressive measures? Did acceptance of American aid increase the political need to stress Communist orthodoxy? Did American aid reduce internal opposition by showing American support for the regime, thereby removing a leadership incentive for reform? These questions, and numerous others that could be asked, suggest that at least some historical generalizations are genuinely truistic, that is, that they are so oversimplified that they are worthless.

There are many impediments to reasonable perceptions of the political and social world. Information that is perceived is filtered through a lens that is at least partly colored by the values and needs of a person. The evidence is much more scanty, much less systematic, and much less precise than in the physical sciences; and we have seen how easily distortion can occur even there. The criteria for determining what is evidence, and the classifications into which it falls, are rarely stated and, at best, are unclear. Problems of selection of evidence and of relating evidence to assumptions or conclusions are often very difficult to solve, even if one makes a conscientious effort. More often, these processes are guided by the conclusions one wishes to arrive at and, even in the case of fair-minded observers, are often reexamined only after the weight of evidence has grossly invalidated prior assumptions. When corrections have been made in one's assumptions, it is often especially difficult to reassess them again when the conditions that required them change again. The demonstrated "falsity" of the original conclusions now bar the way firmly to a reexamination of the evidence, and the parameters on which the original change rested are often overlooked. Only an optimist would be sanguine about this process. Yet, despite all the distortions imposed by values, hopes, and fears, there are methods for transcending such distortions.

Comparative evidence is extremely important for objectivity in the social sciences, precisely because our theory sketches—when these are articulated well enough to deserve even such lukewarm denotation— are so poorly related to boundary conditions, and because the ability to use evidence for confirmation or falsification is so poorly developed. Although physical scientists also gain knowledge comparatively as they learn about boundary conditions, the state of knowledge in the physical sciences provides a warrant for the belief that they have been reasonably success- ful in articulating boundary conditions. The self- conscious pursuit of comparative knowledge in the social sciences, however, is necessary to avoid an unjustified confidence resulting from the observation of properties that are dependent upon a temporary concatenation of variable boundary conditions.

Choices in Ambiguous Situations

If history is ambiguous and full of traps for the unwary, it is natural that statesmen will search for prudential rules to govern conduct. One such rule is to base policies on the capabilities, rather than the intentions, of another state. Yet this also is an elliptical expression that needs careful qualification. We do not station large forces on the borders with Canada and Mexico, because we are quite convinced that they have no intention of attacking within foreseeable circumstances. Despite the French policy that was at one time announced by General Ailleret of *tous azimuts,* no American president took it as a serious possibility that France was going to make a nuclear attack on the United States. The probability that the Soviet Union or China would attack the United States with nuclear weapons was also extremely low, but not so low that any prudential government would entirely discount it or permit either to acquire a first-strike potential if a reasonable option is available. Moreover, although it is difficult, but not impossible, to envisage circumstances in which the deterioration of the American armed forces would incline Mexico, Canada, or France to attack another state, it is much less difficult to anticipate circumstances in which the deterioration of American armed force might lead the Soviet Union or China to attack either some third state or even possibly the United States.

Thus the supposed rule must be treated with circumspection; it should perhaps be reinterpreted as a theorem of excluded choice. We might then read it to state that in those cases in which the possibility of hostile behavior is so low that it can be excluded for practical purposes, one pays no attention to the capabilities of other states. On the other hand, in those cases in which the possibility of hostile action cannot be excluded, one gives significant weight to their capabilities, for there are reasons to expect an interaction between capability relationships and intentions.

Even with respect to the relatively open American political system, fantastic misinterpretations are sometimes made. For instance, General MacArthur is accused of contravening orders in crossing the 38th parallel and in approaching the Yalu River in Korea by President Truman in his memoirs, by such a respected scholar as Robert E. Osgood in his book *Limited War,* and, as late as 1966, by a journalist, C. W. Borklund. Yet, as the paraphrased cablegrams revealed in the Far East hearings of 1951, he acquired previous permission in both cases. It obviously would be a severe mistake to base very important policies—particularly weapons decisions involving long lead times—on tenaciously held dogmas or "inside information" concerning state intentions, although many decisions necessarily involve political judgments.

Of course, if it were possible to state with greater exactitude the relationship between intentions and capabilities and if it were possible to have greater knowledge concerning the intentions of other states, we might well dispense with the theorem of excluded choice or, alternatively, of constrained choice. Unfortunately, there are many circumstances in which neither is the behavior of powerful and important states sufficiently constrained nor are hostile alternatives sufficiently excluded for any great reliance to be put on an analysis of intentions.

I have made a careful study, for instance, of the Czechoslovak coup of 1948. This coup could be interpreted, as it was at the time, as part of a plan that the Soviet Union had in mind from the end of the Second World War. It was possible to show, however, that it could also be interpreted as a situational reaction to the instabilities of the postwar situation, to the fact that the United States and the Soviet Union were the only potential foes of significance, to the need to organize respective spheres of influence, and to the buildup of the Western zones of Germany. It was not possible on the basis of existing information to choose between these hypotheses. Moreover, since most events are overdetermined, it is possible that both motivations played a role; it is also possible that different persons in the Russian decision-making process supported the coup for different reasons. Moreover, it is also possible that even if the motivation to absorb Czechoslovakia within the Soviet sphere was related to situational constraints rather than to an intention to attack Western Europe, Soviet success in this venture might have emboldened it to strive for larger targets in the absence of Western countermoves. Even if the ruling faction in the Soviet Politburo were not so encouraged, potential coalitions to replace it might have formed on the basis of an argument that opportunities were being overlooked. Thus, in this kind of murky atmosphere, to have made decisions based upon analyses of Soviet intentions would have been to gamble recklessly with American security.

In situations of this kind, wise policy makers can observe certain rules of prudent behavior. They can attempt so to act that they exclude the Soviet alternatives they most dislike. They can attempt to constrain Soviet objectives in such ways that the Soviet Union is forced to choose objectives that are liked or that are least disliked by Americans. They can test Soviet behavior in minor ventures to see whether bargains can be reached that can change for the better the matrix within which action occurs. A strategy of this kind, and we are dealing essentially with a strategy rather than with an interpretation or explanation, does not treat the existential world as if it possesses clearly delineated characteristics.

It is difficult for any government to maintain such an open-ended view of the world, for there are constraints upon the decision-making process that tend to inhibit it. For instance, it was difficult for President Kennedy during the Cuban missile crisis, in a matter that might have involved nuclear war, to admit to himself that he was essentially testing a highly ambiguous foe that might have behaved in response to his moves in ways considerably different from his expectations. Although Kennedy was sophisticated in this respect, in general leaders feel much more assurance psychologically when they are presented with authoritative interpretations and explanations of the behavior and intentions of other countries or of their leaders, particularly when nuclear destruction may hang in the balance. Advisers who suggest that one guess is as good as another risk their credibility. Although Kennedy did have the rule of keeping options open—a rule more appropriate in some kinds of situations than in others—it nonetheless remains true that there is a psychological imperative to reduce uncertainty and that this often interferes with appropriate strategic conduct in international relations or in other political behavior.

On the other hand, the assertion that intentions are uncertain does not mean that all aspects of behavior are uncertain. Although the Soviet Union has changed greatly over time and although the characteristics of Russian bargaining behavior may change, there are, in the absence of strong evidence to the contrary, certain observable Russian bargaining characteristics —they may be general Communist bargaining characteristics—that any wise government would take into account. According to Sir William Hayter, as reported by Dean Acheson, bargaining with the Russians is "like putting a coin in an old-fashioned penny-in-the-slot machine. Sometimes you got what you wanted, but usually not. Sometimes you got nothing at all. It helped from time to time to shake the machine and sometimes to kick it, but it never helped to argue with it." Although Sir William undoubtedly meant this description in a metaphoric sense, it does convey significant information about Russian bargaining behavior that any sensible government would take into account. This is an issue entirely separate from that of intentions; it represents historical knowledge of style about which greater assurance can be held, even though this information also can become invalid over time.

How one behaves in the face of uncertainty depends upon a number of considerations. This is a subject treated in the strategic literature and about which I have written elsewhere.[4] A few simple remarks will have to suffice here. For many significant actors prudence is a good rule for behavior. To the extent that the existing situation is reasonably

4. See "A Note on Game Theory and Bargaining," in Morton A. Kaplan, editor, *New Approaches to International Relations,* pp. 483ff. The subject is also discussed in *System and Process in International Politics* (New York: John Wiley & Sons, 1957), pp. 167ff.

satisfactory, and it would require a good amount of comparative historical evidence to suggest the contrary for the most important states in the world arena, one does not risk the existing situation for small gains on the basis of tenuous judgments. This is particularly true if one thinks that history is on one's side. When Stalin referred to certain demands by the Yugoslavs and Bulgarians with respect to the Balkans as involving a Comsomalist preventive war policy, he was not likely indicating a distaste either for war or the extension of Communism. He likely thought merely that Russia's historical prospects were too good to justify that kind of risky policy.

On the other hand, with a different view of history, even a great state may be led into risky adventures. If one believes, as Hitler and Mussolini believed, that fortune governs the world and that opportunities then existed that would not recur for a thousand years, then gambles become justified. This is particularly true if one has a romantic notion of history that seeks for authenticity and that denigrates thought and calculation.

Sometimes, moreover, states are in desperate situations where only gambles against enormous odds can save them. Czechoslovakia found itself in such a situation in the spring crisis of 1938. It won that gamble but its fate was sealed nonetheless. It is in the nature of such risky gambles that they usually fail.

On the other hand, Schumpeter's evidence with respect to businesses and social classes seems to indicate that those that do not grow decline, that there is in general no such thing as mere stasis. Sometimes growth occurs as part of a risk-taking process, although recently in business operations, large corporate agglomerations appear to reduce risks and business efficiency while increasing stability through diversification and increased financial resources. Although we do not know the boundary conditions on which this has been dependent, in the international system, growth has tended to involve the taking of risk. Historically it has been the adventurous state that has expanded. Usually states, unless protected by geographic insulation, as in earlier ages, enter a period of decline and of increased risk when they retrench. A distinction, therefore, probably deserves to be made between the huge risk policies of a Napoleon or of a Hitler and the more mildly expansive or risk-taking behavior that seems consistent with maintained national stature.

There is another line of behavior open to states that has already been alluded to. In addition to constraining alternatives for potential opponents, states may attempt to change the nature of the system within which choice is made. Game theoretic devices can serve as metaphors for such existential problems. Although the criteria for the identification of the variables or for the discrimination of their values are poor, nonetheless the metaphors can have an appropriately profound influence on decision-making for their use may involve, not so much a decision concerning what the situation is, as a decision concerning the direction in which it should be transformed.

For instance, it is not clear that the early stages of the nuclear arms race genuinely constituted a prisoners' dilemma; nonetheless the lack of resemblance was not sufficiently great for comfort. Both Russia and the United States acting independently were able to transform the situation through the development of solid-fuelled and storable liquid-fuelled missiles. Sometimes it requires explicit and direct cooperation to change a situation; in some cases cooperation may be exceptionally difficult. The problems of inspection required to prevent the development of MIRV (Multiple Independent Re-entry Vehicles) or its installation appear exceptionally large, as do the problems of inspection required to deter qualitative changes in weapon systems, such as the opening of scientific laboratories in both Russia and the United States to nationals of the other country. Sometimes these difficulties can be overcome and the situation transformed; and sometimes they cannot, in which case one must live with the potential instabilities of the existential situation.

Much of the historical process involves not so much an interpretation or an explanation of what the historical situation is existentially, although often people believe this is what they are doing, as creative transformations of situations in order to reduce particular uncertainties through the creation of shared expectations. This is a continual process, for solutions introduce new uncertainties as the circumstances of systems change. Nonetheless, much of what passes for history involves the interpretation of the past from the standpoint of the creative present. We thrust upon the past that perspective which succeeds in dominating the present insofar as it constitutes a solution for the problems of the present; much of historical interpretation involves successive phases of this process. This does not mean that there is not such a thing as truth with respect to the past, but it does imply that adequate historical research requires an openness to the nature of the process rather than a closure to the process resulting from particular dogmatic retrospective interpretations.

If anything is called for, it is the emphasis of ambiguity. Information is filtered through perspectives. Much is not directly available—the beliefs or motives of other people, for instance. Moreover, people distort their own motives. Our explanations are based on theory sketches at best. We seldom have any good method for comprehending different theory sketches (perspectives) as they apply to the same set of outcomes or problems. Our inadequacy in enumerating boundary conditions and confirming or falsifying evidence makes it easy to "fudge" evidence to fit our preconceptions. When we quantify evidence, we often quantify that which is quantifiable rather than that which is relevant. Our criteria for evidence are often very poor. It is almost enough to make one despair of the concept of historical truth.

Properly used, however, successive historical experiences provide wider frameworks within which more objective historical interpretation is possible. Each new social existential experiment, for this is what each historical epoch is, provides a wider frame of reference for the interpretation of the past. Just as the history of science permits more general theories, or at least more adequate semigeneral theories, than were available in the past, so greater experience with comparative human behavior provides a wider potential net for the interpretations we can place upon this behavior.

Since all knowledge is context-determined, we can never reach out to complete an ultimate "true" interpretation; but we can overcome the limitations of past interpretations, provided we maintain our openness to ambiguity, by making use of wider and wider comparative perspectives. If objective historical truth is viewed, not within the constrictive framework of a copy theory of knowledge, that is, of an independently subsisting and copiable reality, but within the framework of pragmaticist relationships, then the infinite experimentation advocated by Peirce provides increasingly deeper and deeper knowledge concerning the historical process.

Quantitative and Qualitative Interpretations of History

There has been a burgeoning of quantitative work in the social sciences in the last several decades and in particular in political science during the last decade. The introduction of quantitative methods, in particular in the area of concept formation, will increase the power of social science. On the other hand, just as there is reason to believe that the microevents of social science are unlikely to become subject to theoretical treatment, it is equally unlikely that the most important facets of macrosocial science will become subject to quantitative analysis.

In the first place, there are no genuinely independently measurable equalities in social science. In the second place, in those aspects of social science where theoretical treatment is more likely, that is, at the level of macrosystem analysis, we cannot run the sorts of repeated experiments that can be run with respect to public opinion studies or other aspects of sociological or political analysis related to microevents. Thus our universe of instances is small and the parameters of the instances change over time in such ways that we cannot fully check the relation of the parameter changes to the system's behavior. Moreover, even could we do this, much of the systems models would be qualitative, with numbers functioning only with respect to certain selected aspects of the system. This could be overcome only if simulation models, not of small groups, but of larger macrosystems, really simulated their dominant variables, if such exist, in a meaningful and analyzable way. Although such simulations may tell us something about the social psychology of decision-makers who operate within small groups, and even here the information would be quite limited, the differences between the small groups used for simulation purposes and the macrosystems they are designed to simulate are significant. Moreover, we do not know either what has produced the results in terms of the information of the participants or which variables of the model are causally sensitive, because the models are too complicated for current methods of analysis.

In the third place, if we deliberately abstract from reality and attempt to simulate theoretical components of macrosystems on computers, we are often forced to use quantitative variables that simplify and abstract from their referent more radically than is true of the variables used in physical theories. They often have no direct external referent. In our computer simulations of "balance of power" systems, for instance, we use fungible military capabilities that are simply substitutable. This introduces no great difficulties to the extent that the model is considered primarily as a model of rational choice and is expected to make predictions with respect to the outside world only insofar as either this simplification does not grossly falsify cases of application or, alternatively, insofar as the relationship of the opposing forces in particular cases can be calculated, despite the fact that the existential elements of military capability are not genuinely substitutable. It is possible to make reasonable judgments about the cases in which this is or is not true. This introduces the fourth difficulty, namely, that the selection of the variables to be quantified depends upon a theoretical sketch that gives meaning to the choice of variables.

Much of the quantitative work in the social and political sciences deals, not with systems, but with such system parameters as votes, trade, diplomatic interchanges, messages transmitted across borders, and so forth, which are measured to give certain impressions of trends over time and of relationships to other gross changes noted within the systems. This can be useful, but its utility depends upon the selection of relevant criteria for the variables. It is not entirely unknown for such variables to be selected for their countability rather than for their relevance to a theoretical sketch. It is also not entirely unknown, for instance, for certain transaction analyses to be carried on without careful attention to the questions designed to be probed by the analyses. This often inadvertent failure obscures the fact that the most important political systems could not be directly studied in this way, for the interchanges and transactions that are so important to the understanding of these systems are usually small in number and differ qualitatively in important ways. Thus, for instance, many of the studies designed to show that the world is no longer bipolar—and this may possibly be the case even with respect to the most important military-political questions—show only that certain kinds of subsidiary regional subsystems display non-bipolar patterns of transactional flow with respect to less central questions. This does not mean that such studies have no merit at all, for they do probe something and do give some indications of sociometric relations as viewed from certain perspectives. But they provide insights only where the flow of micro-transactions is reasonably large—something that is often not the case with respect to the most important kinds of transactions, where usually only qualitative information can provide the deepest insights—and they appear to say more about the macrosystems than they do. This can often be misleading.

Attempts to deal with the empirical aspects of political and historical life quantitatively, even at the parameters of systems, usually involve data that are overdetermined. Thus spurious or misleading correlations or factor loadings often show up in such data. For this reason, it is usually unwise to accept such quantitative data unless a qualitative explanation sketch can also be offered. For instance, Hayward Alker finds a relationship between trade and United Nations voting on supranationalism for the Arab and Latin nations. However, as Arthur Burns points out, it is difficult to see why high trade with Western nations, in particular, with the United States, the United Kingdom, and France, is associated with supranationalist voting by the Arabs and Latins, especially since France was dubious about United Nations supranationalism in any event.[5] In general, trade with the United States had little correlation with United Nations supranationalist voting. On the other hand, Burns points out that the Arab states gained from the United Nations' handling of the 1956

5. Arthur Lee Burns, "Quantitative Approaches to International Politics," in Morton A. Kaplan, editor, *New Approaches to International Relations* (New York: St. Martin's Press, 1968), pp. 193ff.

Suez crisis and that this experience provides a good qualitative ground for explaining their voting pattern. Moreover, he believes that the fact that the correlation would presumably have come as a discovery to the Arab delegates, who would have been very unlikely to connect trading with the West with their voting in the United Nations, is at least inconvenient for the conclusion Alker reaches. Although factor loadings or correlations may confirm qualitative theories or may serve as the foundation for the development of qualitative theories—and even this is dubious—it is unlikely, and perhaps impossible, that they will provide acceptable explanations by themselves. This example helps to illustrate why most social science theorizing will likely remain qualitative and comparative.

The role of qualitative approaches will be great with respect to microevents, such as political decisions, when they are treated, not as part of a distributional sample, but as single events to be explained in their own terms. In the physical sciences, Boyle's laws, for instance, tell us something about the physical distribution of gases in a confined space. They do not tell us what a particular particle of gas will be doing; to the extent that it is possible to account for this, one has to make a particular analysis of the impact of other particles upon the specific particle of gas the path of which is to be explained. In applying the theorem of restricted choice to a political question, the weaving of the web of evidence will be largely qualitative, although numbers may play a role in the determination of individual constraints. Thus, for instance, in analyzing the superiority of the American strategic force over the Russians at the time of the Cuban missile crisis, the numbers of weapons, the size of the warheads, the accuracy of the vehicles, and so forth, are essential to the determination of the superiority. It is nonetheless important to recognize that even here much of the strategic theory that gives meaning to the numbers is qualitative. In the theoretical treatment of macropolitical systems, qualitative statements of the relationship between the structural elements of the political system and the ways in which certain kinds of demands are processed and needs satisfied and the ways in which the structures and processes differ between different types of political systems will prove much more important than quantitative measures.

Parameter measures may provide information concerning threshold phenomena: for instance, a person with a temperature above 110° F. will die. But variability in political and social systems is much greater than in physiological systems, and we will likely need to start with qualitative explanations. To understand political integration, for instance, we will need to examine role opportunities and costs, among other things, to understand why it is not unlikely in some circumstances and is unlikely in others. Parameter measures are more likely to be useful as supporting evidence for such system propositions than as independent measures. Much of the quantitative work in political science has actually diverted political science from political analysis, both of a macro and of a micro character.

Political macroanalysis involves a study of role interrelations within a systems framework. It usually involves equilibrium analysis, although there may be applications that involve specific parameter effects or intersystem interactions. Political and historical microanalysis is inherently applied research. It focuses on individual personality outputs as they respond to specific parameters and specific role requirements in different systems. Even where the statistical treatment of classes of individuals is attempted, the foregoing remains true, although in this case the research abstracts from individual motivation. In both cases, however, one must analyze the relations of motivation and action within the framework of opportunities and costs if the measurement of parameters is to provide adequate supporting evidence. Although independent parameter measures may provide some clues either because of rate or direction of change or because they suggest that a threshold has been reached, such measures are at best supplementary. It is therefore unlikely that a particular quantitative measure of a parameter will have significance across different kinds of systems or even within a particular system over time. As population changes, as expectations and political experience change, and so forth, what would have been significant at one time might well not be significant at another.

The qualitatively trained observer who knows how to make appropriate identifications will usually be better off than the person who depends upon numbers, although the person who can combine both techniques adequately will obviously be better off still. Similarly, at the microlevel of analysis, the person who understands the morale and leadership of a military force will do better in predicting its behavior than one who merely counts the number of guns and planes it possesses, although again a person who can combine both techniques will do better yet. Nonetheless, the point I am attempting to make retains its relevance; the social sciences and history will most likely remain much more qualitative and comparative than the physical sciences. Thus historical, political, and social interpretations and explanations of important events or decisions and of general macrosystem behavior will be largely qualitative.

We have reason to be suspicious of those who use coding devices to determine the authors of plays or the painters of pictures. The results will be no better than the codes we begin with. Precisely because recognition problems are among the most difficult to solve, it is unlikely that we have yet learned how to code adequately. Thus it is unlikely that such methods can yet supplant qualitatively trained experts, although, in some cases, they may be of supplementary value.

Is Social Science Value Free?

There is much talk today by some radicals to the effect that social science should not be value free. They are seldom explicit in their arguments, but it seems to me much of the previous discussion is relevant to this question. I do not know of any social scientist who does not believe that some outcomes in the real world are better than others. There are surely few social scientists who are unaware that the very choice of which projects to carry out involves some kind of value choice, if only with respect to what interests them or to what advances their professional career (or to some other criterion).

On the other hand, surely radicals do not contend that a situation in which someone argues that "the revolution" will occur merely because he desires it has anything at all to do with the intellectual search for truth. It is ridiculous, for instance, to claim that generals are nuclear madmen simply because this characterization fits a particular value schema better. (If radicals want to use social science, not as a means to knowledge, but as a lever in a revolution, different issues arise.)

Marx's theory of value was in some ways one of the most important props of his economic theory. Yet, it is universally recognized as false today, and no serious scholar would suggest resurrecting it because it is useful propaganda. The elements in Marx that survive—and that make him one of the great figures in the history of human thought—are those elements about which we can achieve some reasonable degree of second-order agreement, even though we may reject the exact form in which Marx proposed them. Whatever the limitations of the class approach to social interpretation, and they are severe, the approach nonetheless does illuminate a number of important perspectives that would be ignored in its absence. Marx turned our attention to some of the important problems of the sociology of knowledge and to the important problem of alienation. The relation of man to his work is surely one of the most important problems facing him and one we have not yet solved in any satisfactory manner.

It is true that some social scientists are unaware that particular voting schemes are related to the numbers and types of parties, the range of opinions represented, or so forth, or that in committee problems, the order of the agenda at times determines the substantive result. To the limited extent this is true, those particular social scientists may be unaware that seemingly neutral practices bias results in determinable ways. Such lack of awareness is not common, however, and is overcome by the development of better "theories" and by the kinds of comparative researches that discriminate boundary conditions. Proof of the existence of this problem requires application of the "neutral" or value-free methods of science.

The assertion that social science is not value free is either a value-free assertion or it is not. If it is not a value-free assertion, its truth cannot be independently confirmed. In this case, the position is as anti-intellectual as were Nazi claims. If it is value free, then it is an implicit admission that at least some generalizations are neutral in terms of methodology, if not in terms of consequences, and therefore in principle are independent of the particular purposes and upbringing of the person who asserts them.

If the assertion that social science is not value free is claimed to be value free, then what kinds of statements are claimed to be not value free? Moral claims, for instance, are obviously dependent on value premises; choices among them depend either on some objective criterion—such is suggested to be possible in my book, *Macropolitics,* or by (but this is moot)

Marx's historical materialism—or on the values one accepts. Even, however, if there is some independent criterion, it need not, and likely will not, allow a univocal settling of claims. If this is what is meant, the argument may be at least partly conceded.

If, however, it is argued that people tend to make claims related to their class or social position, this is a statement that can be subjected to empirical analysis. Evidence either supports this proposition—it is not yet an explanation—or does not. This is so obviously the case that it can hardly be what is claimed.

It may perhaps be the case that something else is really being claimed, even if it is not well stated. There are no social science theories—only theory sketches, and not many of these. Their variables are poorly identified, their boundary conditions poorly stated, and the evidence required for confirmation or falsification difficult to state or to find or to evaluate. In such circumstances, it is easy to select evidence that supports explanations one prefers. That this occurs —that it may even be the rule—is a confirmable value-free proposition. To view this state of affairs as a regulative principle for social science would be to accept the practices of the confidence man as a guide to scientific practice.

There may, however, be another, but related, sense in which the principle is asserted. It may be argued that many social scientists present status quo supporting but inadequate theories as scientific proofs. It may even be argued that an interlocking directorate of foundations, corporations, and universities determines the direction in which social science goes and even the subjects it explores. Either or both of these charges might be correct either in whole or in part; yet it is difficult to see how these charges can be investigated or assessed except in the value-free sense.

Moreover, although social scientists with anti-status quo values may feel a particular need to challenge so-called status quo social science, it is important for them to distinguish two roles. The first role is that of the social scientist. The regulative principle of social science should be that of science. Despite the temptations to misuse techniques, despite the ease of doing so and the difficulty of reaching scientific conclusions, scientific and comparative method is essential both for learning about the world and for revealing how some have misused the methods of science.

On the other hand, in arriving at social policy, we seldom have time to wait for science to speak. Here, our values often properly guide us in reaching our decisions in the face of uncertainties. There are no sure guides here, although there may be some useful rules of thumb. For instance, forty million people died in the Second World War. Had Nazi conquest been accepted, except for passive resistance, far fewer would have died, and the Nazi regime might have mellowed from within. We do not know this to be wrong, but there is little in past experience to validate it, and the Nazis clearly constituted a horror. Moreover, it was not clear that so many people would die. Whether the governing rule of thumb—that of opposing an evil nation on the verge of obtaining international predominance — was a good or bad one, it clearly was value loaded. It is important to recognize this but not to confuse it with a question of scientific method. And even in those cases in the area of political decision that are value loaded, it is important to assess as objectively as one can those facets of the situation that are susceptible to analysis. Whatever one thinks of America's basic goals with respect to Vietnam, for instance, the inability in the period 1961–63 to recognize the inadequacies of the Diem regime and the then poor prospects for the counter-guerrilla war led to failures in choice that almost no one will attempt to justify today.

It is not true that study of the present and the past, particularly from a comparative point of view, necessarily produces justification of the present any more than it necessarily produces cultural relativism. Whether individuals who prefer to study the present tend to be quietists or those who prefer comparative work tend to be relativists is a separate, and value-free, issue. Although Marx is correct in asserting that one way to learn about the social world is to change it, few would care to justify either the Nazi or Stalinist regimes on this ground. Such "experiments" are not closed laboratory experiments that can be varied at will; and they impose real—and often irreversible—costs on real people. Overemphasis on this Marxian view ignores the ignorance and ambiguity in the social sciences and in fact implicitly prejudges issues from a global and predetermined perspective, for Marx, in effect if not in intention, answers many of his questions in advance on the basis of his definitions.

The Marxian view that conflict occurs where classes do exist and harmony where classes do not exist, is incompatible with modern social science. It fails to distinguish properly between pure conflict, pure cooperation, and mixed situations. It is simplistic, useless for analytical purposes, and moralistic. It imposes its value loadings on inquiry in advance of the inquiry, reifies the concept of class, and defines away innumerable causes of potential conflict. The simple, and purely analytic, truth that two independent variables cannot be maximized simultaneously is foreign to Marxian analysis. The prejudice of the vulgar Marxists, including C. Wright Mills, to the effect that equilibrium analysis is incompatible with the recognition of conflict is merely ignorant of the fact that there are equilibria, although not necessarily univocal ones, in many conflict situations. It also fails to distinguish between closed theory sketches and their applications and therefore derives inaccurate conclusions. Indeed, in many cases, change can be produced and controlled only by learning the conditions for the maintenance of a given equilibrium. Much of classical Marxian analysis is based upon a claim to demonstrate that the conditions that support capitalistic processes (equilibrium) change over time in a way inconsistent with long-term equilibrium. In this case, the two elements are so closely related that the equilibrium Marx analyzes can be regarded as "unstable" on a secular basis. But surely such a conclusion is subject to confirmation; it is not merely to be asserted on the basis of a "theory." It is the world that determines the truth of theories and not the truth of theories that determines the world, as Marx himself asserts in his glosses on Feuerbach.

3
Freedom in History

Freedom and Indeterminacy

What is it that constitutes freedom either for an individual or for a social organization? Some talk of freedom as if it were an absence of determination—as if it represented the individual's lack of conformity to a predictive mold. In a sense, individuals always do overflow our predictive models. In the Peircean sense, no series of experiments can ever exhaust the meaning, that is, the properties, of an entity. There are always residual elements left out of account by the categories we apply.

Even in the area of macrophysics, where we appear to know universal laws of nature, we are nonetheless never absolutely certain what these laws are. As Peirce says, the laws of nature may themselves be changing and, although we can bring such changes within the framework of a new law, we can never reach anything that could be called absolute truth.

When we come to the area of the social sciences, this problem becomes much worse. No single theoretical sketch exhausts those aspects of a situation or of a personality in which we are interested or is adequately related to boundary conditions. Even in those cases where a particular theoretical perspective seems dominant, this dominance is not complete and leaves much out of account. Even with respect to the compulsive-obsessive character type, whose behavior is extremely stereotyped, there are subterranean processes that are not apparent to us that will eventually produce surprises for others and for the person himself.[1]

When we try to engineer for a variety of theoretical perspectives, perhaps through the theorem of restricted choice or the theorem of excluded choice, practically, we have no theoretical perspective from the standpoint of which we can assess accurately the importance of the elements. We also have a problem of identification of the variables and of the criteria for them. The theoretical grounds for such choice are less than completely compelling. The extent to which the real existential situation can slip away from the universal categories designed to explain them attains major significance in the area of individual and organizational behavior. Thus there is a real but misleading element of truth in the claim that freedom

1. I am not arguing that such events cannot be explained or even that they are in principle unpredictable. There will, however, always be limitations of knowledge and of individual theoretical perspectives.

exists to some extent in our lack of constraint by deterministic theoretical schemes; to attempt to fit human beings or organizations within categories is to ignore the degree to which categorizations are distortive. Moreover, there is reason to believe that obsessive-compulsive individuals who constrain their own behaviors in terms of stereotyped beliefs, and who lose contact with their own biological and psychological mainsprings, do deprive themselves of freedom.

To the extent that the existential world escapes our categories, our knowledge of some properties of events is contingent. Perhaps this is what Heraclitus meant by flux—contingent deviation from law or justice. Would we assert, however, that the indeterministic particles of subatomic physics are "free"? Schrödinger's equations can be viewed as laws; however, even if, or especially if, subatomic particles are lawless, it would be difficult to say what we mean by "their freedom."

The statements that we can make about the existential world are indeterministic when either the measurement error or the induced experimental perturbation is relevantly large when considered within the context of what it is that we want to explain or to predict, or when ignored or otherwise unknown parameters affect behavior, as in coin tossing or in the decay rate of particles. When none of these cases hold, then I believe that for all practical purposes our explanations are deterministic. Every theory in physics—determinate and indeterminate—is itself a scientific universalistic type of statement at the appropriate metalevel. In the case of quantum mechanics, this is true at the level of Schrödinger's equations in which velocity and position are not simultaneously meaningful.

If this is correct, then something of a similar, although surely not identical, order can be stated about so-called indeterministic freedom in the social and political world. We have no right to confuse the perhaps inherent limitations of scientific technique with an independent characteristic of the phenomenon being investigated or to draw the conclusion that these limitations, whether residual or fundamental, constitute part of the meaning of freedom.

One may perhaps interpret the same phenomenon from a somewhat different perspective. One might speak of the freedom of the individual as residing in his partial opaqueness to predictive schemata, even those employed by the individual himself, for individuals do occasionally surprise themselves. In this sense, the assertion of human freedom would not be an assertion of an inherent inapplicability of law but rather of pragmatic limitations on such applicability. In this sense, the assertion of freedom would constitute an implicit attack on unambiguous categorization—as assertion that personality or even organizational behavior overflows and at times even confounds the categories we set up for explanatory purposes. There is much to be said for this perspective, but on the other hand it is difficult to believe that it plumbs the depths of the concept of freedom. Freedom would then reside, if not in the lawless, at least in the unexplainable and the unknowable. The more a man was a mystery to himself, the freer he would be. The less moral rules or conscious choice guided him, the freer he would be. But we do not need to engage in these paradoxes. We mistake operational limits for self-subsisting existential characteristics. We fail to distinguish discovery—or the process of reaching a conclusion—from the laws, theories, or theory sketches employed in legitimating it. We make an inappropriate use of the distinction between open and closed systems.

The biologist, Bertalanffy, speaks of biological systems as "open" and as thereby contrasted with closed physical systems. However, all scientific models, whether biological or physical, are necessarily closed and complete; and all existential worlds including even those of physics are necessarily open and inexhaustible. We have already spoken of the fact that a physical experiment depends upon a number of "ifs," namely, the parameter conditions assumed to hold for the physical experiment. These conditions obviously can vary without the knowledge of the experimenter, although in most physical experiments they do so with a reasonably low probability. There is, however, another sense in which all experiments or all decision processes are open. The conscious present, the arena within which the known is known, is never part of scientific closure. The decision-maker can take his motivations into account but, insofar as they are taken into account, they are still contemplated within that "moment" of the present that itself is not part of the scientific account. There is, of course, an infinite regressus here, although not a vicious one in Russell's use of that term. Yet that "moment" of the present is not part of the causal chain and, although it can be brought within the chain, there is always another "moment" of the present that is outside of it. In this strictly limited sense, the decision-maker is free of the chain, for however carefully he extends his chain of consideration, he always possesses ultimately a vantage point that is outside of it. The existential world is an open world. Since the past can never be completely described and since the future can never be completely predicted, these also lead to the same conclusion.

However, knowledge and communication depend upon closure. The world of knowing is open; the world of the known is closed. The world of knowing is the world of continuing interaction. The world of the known is the world of closed scientific explanations and of analytic truths.

Freedom and Physical Constraint

Sometimes freedom is approached from a negative point of view: one is free when one is not externally constrained. According to Hobbes, only external physical constraints such as chains curb freedom; threats, including the threatened use of weapons, do not curb freedom, as the individual is physically free to act despite the threat. The two types of situation are clearly different. Nonetheless, Hobbes's usage is not satisfactory. One can escape from chains at least under some circumstances or at times evade them in other ways. Yet someone who points a gun at a man has changed the external environment for him. The man does not have the same choices either in terms of decisions, properly articulated, or of consequences after the threat that he had before; therefore, the threat has changed the ambit of his freedom.

Although the distinction between physical and intellectual or moral capability is useful, it is misleading to equate freedom or liberty only with the absence of external physical constraint. Does, for instance, an Englishman have freedom to be Chinese in the cultural sense? No external physical constraint prevents him from adopting the cultural patterns of China; yet it is vain to suggest that he is free, or at least fully free, to make this choice because there is no physical impediment. It seems much more reasonable to suggest that freedom can be manifested in many different ways and that it can be constrained in many different ways. One will still wish to distinguish between these modes of expression or of constraint, and such distinctions have genuine importance; but it is futile to claim that any particular mode exhausts the concept of freedom.

Freedom is a contextual and relational concept. There is no such thing as freedom in general. Useful distinctions concerning freedom can be made by distinguishing different kinds of entities from man, to whom Ashby's concept of multistability will be (nonexclusively) applied. This concept will also be useful later in this chapter when discussing questions of moral choice and freedom.

Freedom cannot be examined apart from the constraints imposed by the characteristics of an entity. A ball on a surface has the freedom to act in accordance with the laws of mechanical equilibrium but not to run along tracks. A railroad train has the freedom under appropriate circumstances to move along the tracks in whatever direction the tracks go. A jeep can move on roads or on rougher terrain. An airplane has the freedom to fly through the air, but an automobile does not. An automatic pilot on the airplane is free to behave in accordance with homeostatic stability. It can correct for deviations from level flight. If the automatic pilot was appropriately constructed so that it could correct for errors in its wiring to the ailerons of the plane, then it would be ultrastable in Ashby's sense. A system with more than one ultrastable part system is multistable.

Animals have freedom to act in accordance with emotional motivations. Human beings can act self-consciously and reflectively, in accordance with intellectual, strategic, or moral considerations. These create a much greater ambit within which freedom has meaning to individuals. The ways in which freedom can make itself manifest are obviously different, and the kinds of constraints that can be put upon it are likewise different. The social, political, historical, psychological, and individual circumstances in which an individual grows up and lives out his life create opportunities for the expression of his freedom and also place upon him constraints that interfere with other expressions of that freedom.

The distinction between physical and intellectual constraints may even break down, for experiences during the first few years of a person's · life do structure his patterns of response, and even perhaps his physiological system, in such ways that his intellectual and moral reasoning processes are either developed and expanded or limited. Would we care to say that a mother who has not interested her child in external stimuli and who has not assisted it to develop its reasoning capacities has not limited its freedom because there was no external physical constraint? And is there perhaps not a consequent physical constraint? Are there not perhaps internal physical constraints in the form of underdeveloped physiological and neuronic structures that result from the previous absence of encouragement? Freedom at this level involves constraints, choices, opportunities, and awareness of each of these.

Is it not perhaps important or even necessary to limit freedom at some stages of life to protect it for other stages? Is not much of the argument over the educational process perhaps an argument between those who would constrain certain aspects of freedom of choice early in the life stages of an individual in order to protect future autonomy and those who view free choice as part of a continuous positive feedback process?

Freedom and Personality

Modern American social science has learned from George Mead that the individual construes his image of himself in his interactions with other people. As this image builds up within an interactive process within a larger society and cultural framework, the self-conceptions that are developed create certain opportunities for the expression of human freedom and also certain constraints upon its expression. Some people find their self-image dominated by what others think; and these people in effect wear masks, for their self-image is not autonomous but is largely reflective. In some cases, these masks are changed either over time or functionally according to opportunity, circumstance, or need. Such individuals lack a sense of self-identity; they are their own fictional constructions. They differ from the compulsive-obsessive type discussed earlier in the sense that the universal images represented in the masks are not deeply imbedded in their personality structure.

Still another pathological type is the psychopath, or perhaps more correctly the sociopath, who for the most part lacks even a mask and who acts largely in terms of self-gratification. Unlike the compulsive-obsessive type, the sociopath appears warm and gregarious; but his warmth is a surface phenomenon. He is deeply destructive of other people. As he lacks a sense of his own identity, he has no respect for others as individual personalities. The sociopath is the extreme of the romantic type.

The various extreme types are cripples. They lack to some degree human freedom. There are limitations that they cannot self-consciously overcome upon their intellectual, strategic, or moral behavior, either in the sense that they lack such components in large part or even entirely or in the sense that they are unable to make proper qualifications for differences in circumstances and environments.

The realm of the moral is a real one, I believe, and those who are constrained in this respect lack an essential aspect of human freedom. I will not here reconstruct the argument I made in *Macropolitics,*[2] although a few brief remarks can be made. I do not argue that the objectivity of morals implies a univocal standard or a standard independent of circumstances. Genuine conflict exists both within the personality system and within society. What is good for the individual depends partly upon what his history has been and what his circumstances are. The ties that bind him to other individuals within a moral community are limited by circumstance and by opportunity as well as by understanding. Nonetheless there is such a thing as moral behavior. And since individuals are also moral beings, part of their freedom—perhaps the most important part—lies in their development in such ways and in their living in such environments that they can give expression to this aspect of their being. In this sense, their freedom lies, not in their ability to overflow the boundaries of deterministic

2. See the introductory essay and the chapters reprinted from Kaplan, *System and Process in International Politics,* for a discussion of the objectivity of moral behavior and of the kinds of tests in principle that give the concept empirical meaning.

explanatory categorization, but rather in their ability to express themselves as the kinds of beings they are, that is, as moral beings. In the classic sense, their freedom lies in their necessity.

The formulations employed in *Macropolitics*—based on systemic pragmaticism—thus bridge the gap between what man is and what he does in a way that is both clearer and sounder than the methods either of phenomenalism or of existentialism. If, for instance, we speak of a man as being honorable, this can mean very little unless we can distinguish honorable actions from those that are not. To call a man honorable implies that he will engage in honorable acts; it is a reference to what he does or what he is likely to do. However, we know that there are conditions that will cause most men, if not all, to behave dishonorably. And, in the case of the exceptions, we could most likely alter that behavior by altering earlier life circumstances, acculturation, or education. It is the linkage of actual choices to potential choices through the devices of perfect information and of alternative life paths and alternative environments as outlined in *Macropolitics* that circumvents the argument that man is merely a product of his circumstances, or that vastly different behaviors are equally "natural." We now have a test in principle at least that enables us to discover what man is through what he does. And, if the test is only a test in principle, at least intellectually it does not suffer from the profound obscurity of the phenomenological approach. It is in principle scientific.

Freedom and Choosing

Part of the seeming paradox of the relationship of freedom and necessity lies in a failure to distinguish between the process of deciding and the decision. The fact that a normal person has a moral capacity implies that moral decisions (as opposed to unconsidered actions having moral consequences) are not made prior to the application of moral categories or rules. Thus there is a process of decision-making (which may be minimal either in extremely simple cases or where the rules are deeply embedded in personality) during which an individual must consider the range of alternative decisions open to him, that is, the range of decisions he is free to make apart from moral considerations. In this sense, he genuinely does not know what decision he will make prior to an examination of the case; indeed he may not even know whether he is genuinely a moral person, for he may surprise himself even with respect to this.

The seeming paradox lies in the ellipses we make when we consider the process of deciding. Thus an individual may say to himself, "I would steal this money as I am tempted to do, for I need it, were I not a moral person." In this process of contemplation, he may even query to what extent he values being a moral person or even to what extent his acting immorally in these circumstances detracts from his character as a moral person in general. During this process of contemplation, his choices are open. They close only as the appropriate constraints are applied.

Some of these constraints may be ephemeral. A particular moral decision may be made because a person was irritated in the preceding ten minutes. It is then possible to say that he would have chosen differently under different circumstances. This is an accident in the sense that it is not predictable merely from knowledge of his personality. Yet, rather than being an expression of his freedom, such a surd is a constraint on it. Choices made on the basis of whims or momentary feelings do not genuinely represent the individual. In this sense, they have constrained him in a way that a more determined decision that resulted from something lying much deeper in his personality and moral system would not have constrained him.

Even these deeper elements, however, appear open to choice before the decision is made. It is only after the constraints are applied, that is, only after the ellipses are spelled out, that the decision becomes determined and follows from personality and circumstances. And it is only when circumstances both external and internal permit the individual to act in accordance with his deepest roots that we can genuinely refer to him as a free individual who has freely chosen to do that which he genuinely wants. We hypothesize that an individual constrained by powerful emotions he cannot control or an individual who is unable to develop and act according to moral standards is not free and probably has some recognition of this lack of freedom. He is subjected to enormous compulsions beyond his intellectual control, or he searches for gratification in a way that denigrates his own moral being, or he is deracinated and operates within a set of universalized standards that are divorced from consideration of circumstances and that fail to interact with his own personality system.

When Marx spoke of the transition from the realm of necessity to the kingdom of freedom, he was, imprecisely perhaps, talking about the need of man to construct an environment that permits greater scope for his intellectual and moral capacities. Whether human history is the march of freedom on earth depends upon the extent to which man can learn how to control his environment in order to decrease his dependence on external constraints. Much of the frustration with modern life arises from the fact that man has succeeded in creating organizational monstrosities that are almost incapable of control either by the mass of men upon whom they operate or even by the elites that apparently sit in control of them.

Freedom and Multistability in Choice

When we speak of constraints as limitations on freedom of the individual, this should not be interpreted in any simple-minded sense. The system of which we are speaking is a complicated multistable system in Ashby's sense and has complicated negative feedback loops. The system thus has a certain capability for correcting itself. To the extent that some of man's capabilities depend on physiological processing and involve neural pathways that can develop only during early stages of life, the corrections that can be made later through the negative feedback system are limited by earlier constraints.

Nonetheless the conception that a particular matter is beyond individual self-control can itself become a factor that limits self-control through its influence upon the informational set and the motivational pattern of the individual. Both the conception that the individual is incapable of moral or intellectual behavior and social patterns that reinforce such lack of capability produce positive rather than negative feedback and worsen the situation. Our typical models of insanity and of social irresponsibility both reinforce positive feedback processes and neglect the potential negative feedback loops.

These models of insanity are closed in a way that leaves out of account important factors, particularly those of information and expectation. It is harmless that the models are closed; this is a reasonable heuristic device that permits the generation of conclusions and the engineering of the closed model to the real, open world. The damage is done when the models are closed in a way that both impedes understanding of existential system operations and introduces social costs greater than are probably necessary. From the standpoint of social utility, it might instead be desirable to make an error of a contrary kind—to assume greater capability for negative feedback control, that is, greater freedom for individuals, than some actually have. If this hypothesis is correct, it does not suggest a single mode of response by society, regardless of conditions, but it does suggest a general set of attitudes that recognize individual responsibility.

In our usage, freedom is related to the capacity for and the quality of action of different kinds of systems. Freedom is related to the types and numbers of responses the system has available for any environment, to its capability to use negative feedback, and to its possession of ultra- or multistability. Freedom is thus a relational concept and not an absolute concept. Freedom has constraint as its reciprocal.

As freedom becomes extended and complex and multifarious, so does the system of constraints become extended and complex and multifarious. The freedom of a ball to roll is dependent on its globular shape. The freedom to act morally depends upon a framework for and a capacity for moral choice. Just as the freedom to roll is inconsistent with a square or rectangular shape, so is the freedom to act morally inconsistent with immoral or nonmoral character. Every freedom requires a set of consistent constraints. These constraints are not mere limitations on the specified types of freedom but are the very grounds for their existence. That they are inconsistent with other modes of existence and with their particular freedoms, whether of a greater or lesser or of a higher or lower mode, is tautological.

The quest for absolute freedom of revolutionaries and of anarchists is a romantic and illogical attempt to recapture infantile feelings of omnipotence. The quest for godhead or for absolute freedom on earth is a disguised death wish; in Hegel's words absolute freedom is as meaningless as quaffing a glass of water or as cleaving a head of cabbage.

Perversions of Freedom

The attempts by totalitarian governments and by supporters of the New Left to legislate or to coerce the moral beliefs of the general population involve (not necessarily conscious) attempts to destroy freedom of the individual, to suppress the diversity of life, and to force social and political processes within the world to conform to sets of narrowly chosen tenets: the moral equivalents of simplistic historical theories. Stasis, absolute freedom, and absolute death meet at Kelvin zero, at which motion stops.

In Thomas Mann's *Magic Mountain,* the intellectual duel betwen Herr Naptha and M. Settembrini is a clash between opposing schemes for death, which differ from each other only in their intellectual guise. Peeperkorn, who ignores this dialogue but lives, represents the life principle that breaks through all attempts to impose rigid logical structures upon the world; Mann, however, achieves no synthesis, for Peeperkorn lacks that degree of intellectual control which is necessary for operating in the world and for recognizing that degree of order that temporarily exists and without which life would be impossible.

Individual freedoms exist, but they are relative and constrained by necessities. Order and disorder, freedom and rule, structure and process, are obverse faces of a common existence in which freedom can increase and reach higher levels of performance as the world becomes increasingly complex. Man's neuronic and biological structure provides the framework within which multistable moral and rational self-regulation are possible. The psychopath and the obsessive-compulsive are opposite dysfunctions of self-regulating systems. Both dysfunctions diminish the freedom of multistable systems, one by removing that framework of order within which freedom has meaning and the other by increasing the level of order to the point where all choices are uniformly determined regardless of environmental differences. Thus freedom too has its left and its right deviations. Self-regulation, the cybernaut, is a helmsman or steersman who must navigate the narrow route between the Scylla of absolute disorder and the Charybdis of absolute stasis. Order and disorder, freedom and control, are polarities bound in a symbiotic nexus, false opposites whose meanings are reciprocally revealed and whose limitations are overcome developmentally through appropriate synthesis in complex systems.